*Hands That Touch*
*Hands That Heal*

# Hands That Touch
# Hands That Heal

THE TRUE STORY OF

## Sister Rosalind Gefre

and Her Pioneering Work
in Healing Touch

Joan Holman

*Sister Rosalind Christian Ministries*
ST. PAUL, MINNESOTA

*Hands That Touch, Hands That Heal*

*Published by*
Sister Rosalind Christian Ministries
149 E. Thompson Ave., Suite 160
West St. Paul, Minnesota 55118.
Phone (651) 554-3013

First edition

Visit the Web site at www.sisterrosalind.org for information about Sister Rosalind schools, clinics, and ministry. E-mails should be sent to: info@sisterrosalind.org.

Cover design by Joan Holman and Janelle Bilewitch
Interior design by Wendy Holdman
Composition by Stanton Publication Services, Inc., St. Paul, MN

Library of Congress Cataloging-in-Publication Data

Holman, Joan.
Hands that touch, hands that heal / Joan Holman
1. Biography 2. Health 3. Spirituality

Library of Congress Control Number 2003105134

ISBN 0-9740530-0-7

Printed in Canada

## DEDICATION

This book is dedicated to all individuals
who are sincerely striving to know and to follow
the spiritual path to which God has called them.

## ACKNOWLEDGMENTS

*My deepest thanks to:*

Sister Rosalind Gefre for entrusting her life story to my hands.

Peter Fahnlander for his inspired leadership
and his great support.

Jodi Taitt, Janie Jasin and Barbara Creswell
for their valuable suggestions and contributions to the book.

Sheryl Trittin for her proofreading and copy editing.

Terry Canady for his beautiful singing voice
and gracious spirit, which has blessed the
Sister Rosalind Christian Ministry prayer meetings.

The dedicated and loving staff of the
Sister Rosalind Schools and Clinics.

# CONTENTS

# Preface

*"Let your light shine before men, that they may see your good
works, and glorify your Father which is in heaven."*

(MATTHEW 5:1–16)

T HIS BOOK SHARES THE LIGHT, the good works and the
journey to wholeness of Sister Rosalind Gefre.

This journey, this movement toward wholeness, has been called
the process of "individuation" by the great Swiss psychologist
Dr. Carl Jung. Jung felt that wholeness is the source of all true
health. In fact, the word health is derived from the old Saxon word
"hal" from which come the words "hale" and "whole." When we greet
someone by saying "hello," we are wishing that person wholeness.

The path to union with God is the path towards wholeness or
health. This path draws to us challenging situations that give us
the opportunity to grow. These situations are often full of pain,
conflict and struggle. Pain is a great motivator. In fact, pain can
force people to make significant changes in their lives because
when people are in pain, they become willing to change.

Episcopal priest and Jungian analyst John Sanford stated in his
book *Healing and Wholeness*:

> *"Individuation is a work, a life opus, a task that calls upon us not
> to avoid life's difficulties and dangers, but to perceive the meaning
> in the pattern of events that form our lives. Life's supreme achieve-
> ment may be to see the thread that connects together the events, the
> dreams, and relationships that have made up the fabric of our exis-
> tence. . . . Becoming whole does not mean being perfect, but being
> completed. It does not necessarily mean happiness, but growth. It is*

*often painful, but, fortunately, it is never boring. It is not getting out of life what we think we want, but is the development and purification of the soul. . . .to be healthy means to become whole . . . the truly healthy person is the person who is involved in the lifelong process of individuation."*

JOHN SANFORD

Sister Rosalind followed God's call to practice healing touch even though it brought upon her shame, humiliation and disapproval and cost her her "happy home," her reputation and the regard of her peers.

When a person follows that inner call from God toward wholeness, that person's life then bears good fruit and blesses the whole community. The good fruit of Sister Rosalind includes many significant accomplishments:

- The establishment of one massage clinic in St. Paul, Minnesota, then a massage school in St. Paul, Minnesota, and then many massage clinics and schools in the Midwest
- Putting massage in its rightful place and making it respectable, not just locally, but throughout the world
- Helping to change ordinances in many cities to allow massage therapists to practice as healthcare professionals
- Training thousands of massage therapists in the Midwest who have positively impacted the lives of countless numbers of people through healing touch

The book shares the difficult experiences in Sister Rosalind's life, experiences that were foundational to her becoming the person she is today. If you ask her if it all has been worth it, she will give you a resounding "yes."

Sister Rosalind's life is an example of how an individual who is faithful to God becomes a great blessing to the community and how, through the path of sacrifice, service, surrender and selflessness, God can transform a diamond in the rough into a stone of great brilliance.

Through touch, Sister Rosalind is bringing the love of Christ to a suffering humanity and nourishing hearts and souls as well as bodies.

In addition to her active life of service in the world, Sister Rosalind has a very rich inner life and is a true mystic. Through prayer and meditation and loving service to others, mystics through the ages have come to understand what Jesus meant when he said, "The kingdom of God is within you." Many private, never before revealed details of Sister Rosalind's mystical experiences are shared in this book.

Sister Rosalind's story is an example of what one person can do when he or she is willing to seek first the kingdom of God and then is obedient to the will of God for his or her life. God has a divine plan for every life, and each of us has the choice to accept or reject that divine plan.

Sister Rosalind accepted the divine plan for her life and many blessings are pouring forth as the fruit of the fulfillment of that divine plan. This book is the record of her efforts, her striving, her suffering, her overcoming and her transformation. Sister Rosalind's story is a source of inspiration and guidance for all.

## YOU ARE CHRIST'S HANDS

Christ has no body now on earth but yours,
   no hands but yours,
   no feet but yours,
Yours are the eyes through which is to look out
   Christ's compassion to the world
Yours are the feet with which he is to go about
   doing good;
Yours are the hands with which he is to bless men now.

TERESA OF AVILA

Now when the sun was setting, all they that had any sick with divers diseases brought them unto him; and he laid his hands on every one of them, and healed them.   (Luke 4:40)

And when the woman saw that she was not hid, she came trembling, and falling down before him, she declared unto him before all the people for what cause she had touched him, and how she was healed immediately.   (Luke 8:47)

And Jesus answered and said, Suffer ye thus far. And he touched his ear, and healed him.   (Luke 22:51)

And besought him greatly, saying, My little daughter lieth at the point of death: I pray thee, come and lay thy hands on her, that she may be healed; and she shall live.   (Mark 5:23)

And he could there do no mighty work, save that he laid his hands upon a few sick folk, and healed them.   (Mark 6:5)

And these signs shall follow them that believe; In my name shall they cast out devils; they shall speak with new tongues; They shall take up serpents; and if they drink any deadly thing, it shall not hurt them; they shall lay hands on the sick, and they shall recover.   (Mark 16:17–18)

SCRIPTURE FROM THE KING JAMES VERSION OF THE HOLY BIBLE

# Introduction

PLEASE TAKE A WALK with me in the journey into the life of Sister Rosalind. As you read of her life, you will understand her ever-growing love and commitment to God. Sister is a woman known for her compassion, her warm hugs and her love of Christ.

Sister Rosalind has faced many betrayals by those whom she has trusted most. Sister Rosalind says, "I do not have the gift of discernment but I have the gift of love. I look for Jesus in all of those I meet."

I have witnessed many obstacles that Sister has overcome. Where many would have failed and lost faith, Sister's faith grew and was strengthened. Sister believes that any work for the goodness of the Lord is continually under attack from people who are misled. She also believes that one must not just talk about the Lord, but walk with the Lord in one's day to day activities.

Sister Rosalind and I have worked together for many years. We have laughed together and we have cried together. The closer I become to Sister Rosalind, the closer I become to God.

While my sister Sue was dying of cancer, Sister Rosalind laid her hands upon me and said, "Give it to the Lord." At that very moment a great burden was lifted off my shoulders and I felt the love and presence of God.

In my opinion, Sister Rosalind is a living saint, and this book reveals her inner and outer walk with the Lord. The fruit of her walk with the Lord has been the manifestation of God's love in the world through the gift of touch.

Peter E. Fahnlander
President, Sister Rosalind Schools
and Massage Clinics

# A Message from Sister Rosalind

I T IS MY SINCERE HOPE that this book will lead you to not focus on me as much as it will lead you to Christ. What I really want is that I might decrease and that Jesus might increase in my life so that you will feel His spirit and His love through this book. That is my whole desire.

I am like everybody. Some day I will die and I will be gone. But my hope is that at any time people read this book in the future, even 100 years from now, they will be put on fire for the Lord.

This book is not me proclaiming me; it is me proclaiming Jesus Christ. I walk and talk with Jesus, and He has been my strength and comfort through many dark days and much emotional pain and suffering.

The path God has called me to has not been easy. When I began practicing massage in 1973, it was looked upon as something dirty. Unlike today, there was not the widespread acceptance of massage, and I was looked down upon and ostracized by many. In 1983, I was humiliated when the Vice Squad shut down my massage center in St. Paul, Minnesota. They said I was operating a "massage parlor" without a license. When this made newspaper headlines, I was asked to move out of the convent that was my happy home. Although I was not expelled from my religious community, I had no other home or place to stay. I felt alone and condemned by many in my spiritual community. Years of pain and suffering followed as I listened to, and was obedient to, the voice of God telling me that

I should devote my life to healing touch. This period of time was truly my Dark Night of the Soul. I had to stand almost completely alone. I felt like I had lost everything. But I could not turn away from the calling that Jesus had placed in my heart, a calling to "feed His sheep" through healing touch.

As I continued to follow my path, it took me into the realm of the business world, a world with which I had no familiarity. My background had not prepared me to start schools and clinics. But the need was there, and I jumped in and filled that need. In fact, I keep looking at my life and I often think I didn't really plan my life. All of a sudden, I was doing massage, and doing it very publicly. And although one room is all I ever wanted, I now have six clinics and five schools.

Being naive in business, I trusted people. Unfortunately, many people betrayed that trust and took advantage of me. The only reason there are many Sister Rosalind Schools and Massage Clinics today is because God has raised up and grown the schools and clinics in spite of my lack of business experience and in spite of tremendous obstacles and setbacks.

It has been my mission and my calling to affirm people and to raise people up through physical touch. The Bible is full of stories of Jesus healing people through touch.

Working in the field of massage has been a challenge. I have had thoughts such as, "Here is this Sister and she hugs everybody, and she even hugs men." When I have these thoughts, I have felt Jesus saying, "You know, this is what you need to do because people need to be hugged. They need to know they are beautiful and loved." And so, I am always hugging people, and I notice such a great response in people, and this positive response is what happens again and again and again when I hug people. And when I give massages, people say, "Oh, you know what, I need a hug." And they fall into my arms, and I am aware of the change that happens in people.

People need to be hugged, they need to be touched. People are "skin hungry" and "God hungry."

I am now aware of how important it was for me to be misunderstood, and I know that I have become very strong because of all I have gone through. And I am grateful if I have made even a small contribution to bringing affirmation and God's love to people through touch.

*Sister Rosalind Gefre*

# Enter the World of Massage

YOU WALK INTO A ROOM. It is totally private. You remove your clothes and lay down on your back on a covered massage table, pulling a clean, warm cotton sheet up over your body so that your head is visible and the rest of your body is fully draped. This is your first massage. You are a little apprehensive. You have carefully chosen Sister Rosalind's clinic. Her massage therapy clinics have been in business for 20 years. You have read about Sister Rosalind, seen her at the St. Paul Saints baseball games, and even heard her speak at your church about the benefits of healing touch. Some of your friends have received massages at Sister Rosalind's clinic and told you it was a positive experience. You know her massage therapists are trained healthcare professionals. They are licensed. You are reassured knowing that they also have a code of ethics.

Music is playing softly in the background. Thoughts are racing in your head. You are trying to relax, but you can feel tension and pain in your back and in all of your tissues as well. You have been having back problems and have been diagnosed with fibromyalgia. You have chronic pain throughout your body. You have been to a chiropractor several times and he has recommended massage as an adjunct therapy treatment.

In walks your massage therapist. You have filled out a form with your health history. She reviews this and asks you about certain health concerns, including past surgeries.

Your massage therapist applies massage oil and gently proceeds with deep, long strokes on your arms. You feel the tension begin to release. She massages your face, your neck, your upper chest and the front of your legs. You turn over, and as she massages your back, your shoulders and the back of your arms and legs, you ask yourself why you haven't done this before. It is so relaxing.

You have heard that some people can start crying during massage and that others open up and share very deep experiences, but you have remained quiet during the entire massage. You have not felt like talking, but when she was working on your back, you remembered an injury from childhood, and how painful it was at that time. You wonder if some of your back pain may be related to that injury.

It takes a while to come back to earth, and you are reluctant to get off the table. Maybe next time you will schedule an hour massage instead of a half-hour.

The benefit of the massage is obvious. There is a reduction in the discomfort from your fibromyalgia and your back feels better. Your massage therapist has also recommended a supplement for fibromyalgia and you are eager to try it. She has told you about a couples massage class that you may want to sign up for with your husband so you can learn to do massage at home.

You have now entered the new world of massage, and there is no going back.

⟜

## Chapter 1

# God's Minister of Massage

*Moving massage from disrepute to mainstream acceptance*

SISTER ROSALIND GEFRE is 73 years old. She is vibrant and energetic. She loves life and she loves people. When you come into the presence of Sister Rosalind, you immediately feel her great joy and a deep level of caring for people. No matter where she goes, whether it is a ball game, a business meeting, a presentation in front of a group or the massage schools and clinics that bear her name, she dispenses genuine, heart-felt and loving hugs to people around her. Everywhere she goes, she hugs. She hugs because she believes that human touch is a holy and healing gift from God.

A whole lot of love and energy is packed into such a little woman, a woman who is less than five feet tall. When you ask her height, she will tell you that she really does not know what it is. Sister Rosalind is not concerned about such things. You see, Sister Rosalind is focused on two things: her spiritual life and her life of helping, uplifting, affirming and comforting others through healing touch. She is strong in her faith and steadfast in her devotion to God, and she is strong in her commitment to being a "Minister of Massage."

People come up to Sister Rosalind everywhere, on the street, in the grocery store, in restaurants. They know of her and her work. Groups of people travel with her on spiritual pilgrimages to holy places throughout the world. She receives letters of gratitude from people who are inspired by her life and work. Once, standing in line at a store, a man excitedly pulled his Sister Rosalind St. Paul Saints baseball card from his wallet and told her he carried it with him everywhere.

Sister Rosalind is more than a local town celebrity. Since 1983, she has been featured as an advocate of massage on radio and television and in newspapers and magazines throughout the world. Sister Rosalind's impact on the practice of massage has been significant. There have been over 2,000 graduates of her schools since she started her first school in 1984. Currently, there are five Sister Rosalind massage schools and six Sister Rosalind massage clinics in two states, employing 150 people. The "Sister Rosalind Christian Ministry" holds public prayer meetings dedicated to healing. She even has her own line of massage and skincare products.

Today, massage is very popular. This was not the case thirty years ago in 1973 when Sister Rosalind first began practicing massage. The courage and tenacity of therapists like Sister Rosalind paved the way through much opposition to bring us the benefits of this increasingly popular mode of healthcare.

Massage as a healing modality was still relatively obscure when Sister Rosalind began practicing it. The word massage was often associated with prostitution. Legitimate massage therapists, by association, were lumped into this category and faced tremendous obstacles.

In the process of walking her spiritual path, which has resulted in making a great contribution to the world, Sister Rosalind has experienced struggle and suffering as well as joy and overcoming. Dr. M. Scott Peck, author of the best-selling book *The Road Less Traveled*, has said about the spiritual journey:

*"As we grow spiritually, we can take on more and more of other people's pain, and then the most amazing thing happens. The more pain you are willing to take on, the more joy you will also begin to feel. And this is truly good news of what makes the journey ultimately so worthwhile."*

DR. M. SCOTT PECK

Sister Rosalind has had a trying journey, and as you read, you will learn about her "Dark Night of the Soul." But out of this Dark Night has come great rewards. She has lived her life as the imitation of Christ and has directly experienced the mystical love and peace of Christ.

What does the imitation of Christ require? It requires commitment, it requires effort, it requires trusting one's own inner experience and disregarding public opinion and the opinion of peers when they counter the direction coming from communion with God through the inner experience. It requires standing completely alone when all seems to be against you.

Sister Rosalind will readily tell you that she is not perfect and her humility is genuine. She is no phony, and she does not minimize the suffering her path has entailed. But she does not carry resentment or anger against God for what she has had to endure to be true to God's calling for her life. And the fruit of her efforts is her "Ministry of Massage," a blessed gift to countless people.

➤

## Chapter 2

# The Backdrop—Massage in America

*Massage was associated with the sex industry*

T O REALIZE WHY Sister Rosalind's work in the field of massage is such an achievement, you will need to understand the hostile environment in which she started doing massage, a hostile environment not only in her own religious community but in the secular community as well.

Since ancient times, massage has been practiced for a variety of healing purposes. However, in 20th century America, massage was associated with the sex industry. This was the atmosphere that Sister Rosalind Gefre entered when she decided to dedicate her life to therapeutic massage in 1973. This was a bold and courageous thing to do for a Catholic Sister. Since many in her spiritual community as well as people outside her community viewed practicing massage as something "dirty," Sister Rosalind carried the burden of judgment and condemnation of her work.

Sister Rosalind was determined to change the sordid image of massage, and many have commented that there was no one better to do this than a Sister.

In 1983, Sister Rosalind made headline news. This happened when she opened a massage center in St. Paul, Minnesota, and was visited by the St. Paul Vice Squad who told her that they were shutting her down for operating a "massage parlor" without a license. The City of St. Paul did not differentiate between massage parlors, massage clinics or massage centers. The city lumped them all together. Massage business operators were required to have a license, a mug shot, and a thumbprint on file at the police station to operate in the City of St. Paul. Sister Rosalind thought this was a ridiculous requirement and surely did not apply to therapeutic massage. She told the Vice Squad that she was a nurse engaging in a totally legitimate healthcare practice, and they said that did not exclude her from their requirements.

Since that time, Sister Rosalind has been instrumental in changing city ordinances to allow licensed massage practitioners to practice therapeutic massage. She has spoken to thousands of people about healing touch. She has been featured in books and magazines and has appeared on television and radio throughout the world, including the Joan Rivers television show in 1991. She has even been flown to California by a Minnesota baseball team to give massages at their convention.

In a *Time Magazine* article from July 29, 2002, "Massage Goes Mainstream," Sister Rosalind was featured as "one of the earliest proponents of massage in Minnesota." The article reported that massage has been steadily growing in popularity in the past few years, with the number of American adults receiving massages doubling from 1997 to 2002. In 2002, seventeen percent of Americans got massages, with the majority doing it to relieve stress and "pamper" themselves. Doctors are also writing prescriptions for patients to receive massages, and some insurance companies are paying for massage services.

The development of the portable massage chair in 1986 allowed massage to move out into the mainstream of shopping centers, places of business, sporting events, health food stores and other locations. Sister Rosalind and her students can be seen giving massages at many locations, including St. Paul Saints baseball games.

Sister Rosalind was one of the first people to establish a Christian-based school of massage in the United States. At the time she established the school, in 1984, there were very few massage schools. Today there are 950 state-licensed massage schools in the U.S., and that number is growing.

With the current widespread acceptance of massage, Sister

Rosalind is now seen as a true pioneer. She has paved the way through uncharted territory, and after many years of sacrifice and difficulty, she has left a great legacy of healing touch for generations to come.

⤝

*Chapter 3*

# Simple Beginnings /
# Daughter of the Prairie

*USA Today featured a cartoon where two men are sitting at a bar.
One man is looking at the other and saying, "You know, it's true.
I've never met anyone from North Dakota either."*

T HE WOMAN WHO would become known as Sister Rosalind
Gefre was born six days after the stock market crash of 1929
in one of the coldest, windiest and least-populated states in the
United States. She was the eighth child of a German-Russian
farming family of thirteen children consisting of eight girls and
five boys. She grew up in a family that spoke German in the home,
ate German food and practiced a German work ethic.

The Gefre farm was located near Strasburg, North Dakota, a
small town in south central North Dakota with a current popu-
lation of 553, whose claim to fame is being the birthplace of the
renowned band leader and television personality Lawrence Welk.
The restored Welk Farmstead, a typical example of German-Russian
settler farms found in North Dakota, is visited by thousands every
year from all over the country.

The early North Dakota settlers faced hostile elements and a
struggle for survival. North Dakota has very hot summers, bitterly
cold winters and winds sweeping across flat, treeless plains resulting in severe winter blizzards. The monthly average temperature
for January is 18 degrees Fahrenheit and the average temperature
for July is 84 degrees Fahrenheit. Farmers struggle with a short
growing season and face the possibility of drought, hail and un-
timely rain reeking havoc with their crops.

A part of America's agricultural heartland, North Dakota was
settled by immigrant farmers primarily from Germany, Russia

and Scandinavia. The backbreaking labor of these early pioneers transformed a frontier wilderness into a beautiful landscape of rich, productive Dakota plains golden with wheat.

German-Russian immigrants came to the United States, traveling to North and South Dakota to set up homesteads. Although they emigrated from Russia, these immigrants were part of a German community that had settled in that country. Many German-Russian men fled Russia to escape induction into the Russian army and traveled to obscure rural places in America for anonymity.

Sister Rosalind, born as Margaret Gefre on November 6, 1929, came into this world at the onset of the Dust Bowl (or the "Dirty Thirties," as the decade of the 1930s is known). This was also the decade of the Great Depression, one of the most devastating periods in the history of the United States.

Life had always been hard for farmers, but life was brutally hard with the drought, unrelenting dust storms and economic depression of the '30s. Already skilled at making do with very little, the Gefre family survived amidst the harsh economic landscape of a devastated farm economy.

Sister Rosalind shares an event that left an indelible impression on her during her early childhood:

> ⟿ "I remember one day when I was still very young. We had let the horses eat and rest at noon so they wouldn't tire out. Of course, we also needed to eat and rest. Most of us went in the yard and laid on the grass. Then we saw grasshoppers coming. They were so thick in the sky that the sun was darkened. A swarm had just gone through the farm and in a half-hour the whole garden was stripped of every plant. I had gone to look at the plants before dinner, and then, suddenly, in practically no time, they were all completely eaten away."

An excerpt from the diary of Ann Marie Low, a woman who lived in North Dakota in the 1930s, paints a vivid picture of the backdrop of Sister Rosalind's childhood environment. Sister Rosalind was four and a half years old at the time of these recorded dust storms.

*"April 25, 1934, Wednesday. Last weekend was the worst dust storm we ever had. We've been having quite a bit of blowing dirt every year since the drought started, not only here, but all over the Great Plains. Many days this spring the air is just full of dirt coming, literally for hundreds of miles. It sifts into everything. After we wash the dishes and put them away, so much dirt sifts into the cupboards we must wash them again before the next meal. Clothes in the closets are covered with dust. Last weekend no one was taking an automobile out for fear of ruining the motor. I rode Roany to Frank's place to return a gear. To find my way I had to ride right beside the fence, scarcely able to see from one fence post to the next. Newspapers say the deaths of many babies and old people are attributed to breathing in so much dirt."*

DUST BOWL DIARY BY ANN MARIE LOW, 1984,
UNIVERSITY OF NEBRASKA PRESS

Further description of the harsh environment of the Dust Bowl on the Great Plains is provided by Caroline Henderson in her book *Letters from the Dust Bowl*:

*"Nothing that you can see or hear or read will be likely to exaggerate the physical discomfort or material losses due to these storms. Less emphasis is usually given to the mental effect, the confusion of mind resulting from the overthrow of all plans for improvement or normal farm work."*

LETTERS FROM THE DUST BOWL BY CAROLINE HENDERSON,
EDITED BY AL TURNER, 2001, UNIVERSITY OF OKLAHOMA PRESS

Up until the age of 10, Sister Rosalind lived in some of the harshest conditions ever experienced in the history of the United States. Farm crops died. Black blizzards emerged from the dust as a result of over-plowed and over-grazed land. These dust storms increased in both number and intensity during the early 1930s. By 1934, great dust storms spread out from the Dust Bowl area, creating the worst drought in U.S. history, covering more than 75 percent of the country and affecting 27 states. Newspapers and magazines recorded the devastation of the "black blizzards" across the plains. Dust storms caused serious and even fatal respiratory problems, a condition doctors called "dust pneumonia." Rain finally brought an end to the drought in 1939, but thousands of people lost loved ones, homes and their livelihood.

## NO BITTER MEMORIES

Sister Rosalind's memories of growing up on the farm during this difficult time show no sign of bitterness or feelings of living in poverty:

➤ "I had a childhood with everything I needed. There was always food on the table, a place to sleep and clothes to wear, even though they were hand-me-downs. Our clothing was always patched, something my mother knew how to do so well, especially the bib overalls in which the knees were always worn out. When she was finished with them, I was amazed how nice they looked. Every fall we got two new pair for school, along with two new pair of stockings, and two new pair of underwear. What a joy that was! We were about one mile from school and walked every day. No matter how cold or deep the snow was, we always walked, in rain or snow.

Only about twice during the winter were we picked up by horse and wagon. When that happened, it was very, very cold. There were usually five of us. We milked and fed the animals and had breakfast and then went to school. After school we did the same thing again, then had supper and washed the dishes. We had no running water so we always had to heat water for everything. The house was cold and some nights the water froze in the house. We used a kerosene stove or wood stove with cow chips or whatever we could find to burn. We never thought we were poor. We learned to work hard for a living and we all worked together.

Our food was very good. Everything was home cooked and we had fresh bread about every other day. The food was simple but so good. All my sisters are also very good cooks. I never liked to cook but at times I had to. I'd rather milk by hand, clean the barn, or work in the field. All the plowing was done by horses. We couldn't afford a tractor until about two years before I left home."

## GROWING UP ON THE FARM DURING THE DEPRESSION

Sharing her experience of growing up on the farm during the Depression, Sister Rosalind says:

➤ "We had nothing. We didn't have any electricity. We had a well indoors but that was only for drinking. We had a cistern provided there was rain. Cistern water was only used for laundry, just to wash. And oftentimes we didn't have enough, especially in the winter, and so we either got well water or we had to carry water from the creek. We had what they called Beaver Creek running through our farm, and the creek water was softer than the well water, and you needed less soap, and we made our own lye soap. We had an outhouse, and we had no phone or running water. And even after I entered the convent in 1948, there still was no electricity at my farm home.

## A TRAGIC LOSS

In her childhood, Sister Rosalind suffered the tragic loss of her father when she was only six years old.

➤ "My father had one box wagon on four wheels that he used to harvest the hay, and another box wagon to harvest the grain. He lifted one from the other by himself and it was very heavy. Two or three men should have lifted it, but he did it by himself because he wanted to spare the children the hard work. Well, one day he overdid it and damaged some heart muscle and after a few days he died. He was only 42 years old. My mom was left to raise us kids. There was no welfare and no relief. We didn't have anything. Mom believed in working hard and we children didn't sit around. There was no TV or anything like that. But there was work. There was always work on the farm, so we just carried on. We did our own gardening and we did lots of canning. There were no deep freezers because there was no electricity. So we canned everything. We had a root cellar and put our vegetables in the root cellar to store up food for the winter. We didn't buy lots of food. We canned everything, fruits, vegetables, and meat as well."

## HARD LABOR

Life on the farm required hard physical labor. The entire family, including Sister Rosalind, worked at various chores, such as gardening, cooking, cleaning the barn, milking the cows, farming and butchering animals.

➤ "Mom bought 500 chickens every year. During the summer, we'd sometimes butcher five chickens at a time, depending upon how large they were. As soon as the chickens were big enough to butcher, we'd butcher them. We were a large family and we oftentimes needed five chickens to feed everyone at a meal. As the chickens grew older we probably only needed two and a half. Butchering chickens was almost a daily routine for us. We also butchered cows and pigs and occasionally a sheep. By fall, we had butchered all the chickens that were left and we canned them. We left about 100 chickens for eggs so we would have enough eggs for us to eat during the winter. And we would occasionally butcher again so we would have meat. Chickens were very important in our lives.

We didn't have a milker. So we milked cows by hand, and by the time I was in my teenage years, we had 45 cows to milk by hand. That was done two times a day, morning and night. I think that readied my hands for massage."

## GRADE SCHOOL

Sister Rosalind attended grade school and often missed school to work on the farm.

➤ "We went to grade school but we often had to stay home and help with the farm until all the harvesting was finished. Sometimes we had to be out in the field and watch the cows all day long so they wouldn't go out in the neighbor's yard. The fields had no fences around them."

Sister Rosalind experienced much difficulty in grade school because she did not speak English.

➤ "We spoke German at home. We didn't even know our names in English. We knew nothing in English. But as soon as we entered grade school, we had to speak English. If you didn't speak English, you were punished. The teacher would put your name on the blackboard, and 'Margaret' was almost always written on the blackboard because the teacher would hear me speaking German. So my name would be on the blackboard for breaking the law, and I would have to write on paper 100 to 300 to

500 times, 'I may not speak German. I must speak the American language.' I had to write it after school when all the school children had gone. And I wrote very, very fast since I didn't want Mom to know. And I think God got me ready for massage because I learned how to use three pencils at the same time. In those days, parents supported teachers when children were disciplined. I think God knew I was going to do massage, so he got my hands ready."

## THE HAPPIEST MOMENTS

Sister Rosalind's happy memories of her childhood included new clothing, Christmas and Christmas presents and a special Confirmation dress:

➤ "Midnight mass was to live for. The singing was heavenly. It lifted my thoughts heavenwards and made me think about how beautiful heaven must be. It was so beautiful that I didn't want to leave church. The church decorations included Christmas trees and we never had a Christmas tree at home. I don't remember anyone having a Christmas tree at home.

But we did get Christmas presents. And those were the greatest moments in my life, to get a little present every Christmas. Small things meant so much because we were very poor. We didn't get lots of things. For Christmas, our great gift would be a new pair of stockings or a handkerchief. These were real big things.

One of my happiest memories was getting my confirmation dress. Our clothing was all hand-me-downs. I don't ever remember, up to my teens, ever getting a new dress. But, for my confirmation I got a new dress. I will never forget it, it was so beautiful. And when I think of a beautiful dress I think of that confirmation dress. It was yellow with ricrac. It was gorgeous. I grew very slowly so I was able to wear the dress for a long time. When I outgrew it, the dress went to my younger sister."

✦

*Chapter 4*

# Early Devotion and Spiritual Influences

*"As a child, I studied the lives of the saints, and I think that is what really built my character because I wanted to be like them."*

S ISTER ROSALIND was a deeply spiritual child. She communed with God whether she was working in the fields or milking the cows. Her prayers became a meditation on God. Her family prayed together daily and encouraged the practice of prayer.

"Prayer was always very, very important to me. I always prayed as a child. I don't remember ever not praying from as far back as I can recall. Every night, when we were finished with the meal, we knelt together as a family and said night prayers and the rosary. We prayed before meals and we prayed after meals. During certain months, such as May and August and during Advent and Lent, we said special prayers.

Now, I am not sure how effective the prayers before meals were because here's the table and there's the food, so we'd hurry up and pray, 'Our Father Who Art in Heaven, Hallowed Be Thy Name.' We raced through the prayers so we could sit down and eat. I think that especially happened when we had chicken since we all wanted a special part of the chicken. I liked the feet, neck and wings.

Prayer has just been a part of my life. When I was working on the farm, I was either singing Jesus songs or I was praying. When I was out in the field, if I couldn't have the rosary in my hand, I usually had it in my pocket. And I would be praying, saying to myself the 'Our Father' or the 'Hail Mary,' but doing it very, very slowly and just meditating on the words 'Our Father, Our Father.' It became like food, spiritual food, for me. So those prayers were said very, very slowly. It could take me a whole day to just say the 'Our Father.' When I was out in the field it was a totally different kind of prayer than when I was ready to jump in and eat a meal."

Although Sister Rosalind spoke German at home, she did learn English at school and could read books. However, the school library was not readily accessible except during school hours, and the nearest town was thirteen miles away. Her family owned a car, but they seldom went to town except to take cream and eggs to sell. Although books were hard to come by, she did get her hands on a Catholic digest that contained the lives of the saints. She eagerly read these stories over and over. The stories captivated her, and she felt especially drawn to Saint Margaret Mary Alacoque.

ᵛ "I read her life over and over and over because I could identify with her. She was uneducated, nobody great in the eyes of the world, but Jesus loved her and chose her out of all in the convent where she was. She became my role model. Like her, I knew I could be a good person and become a saint even if I was not educated, even if I was just a farm girl. She was a missionary. Jesus used to appear to her. Just reading about her and thinking about her made my heart come alive. I felt a greater love for Jesus when I read her life. She was always very, very important to me. My baptismal name was Margaret, and for confirmation I took Mary, Margaret Mary because of my love for Saint Margaret Mary Alacoque."

Saint Margaret Mary was visited by Jesus, who asked her to spread devotion to his Sacred Heart. After much opposition, she was successful in doing this and was eventually canonized by the Catholic Church. Perhaps through the life of her patron saint, Sister Rosalind was getting a glimpse of some of the coming struggle and great success she was also going to achieve in her own life.

~

Chapter 5

# The Call to God

*"So I had to write him and say, 'Sorry, sweetheart, but goodbye.'"*

MARGARET GEFRE continued to live and work on the farm throughout her teenage years. She developed an interest in boys and had boyfriends, and one boy in particular had finally captured her heart. She was 18 years old and had met the love of her life and felt that this was the man for her. However, she also was feeling a strong call to religious life. She had to make a choice.

"It was a very hard decision to make since I had met the man that I just knew would be my husband. But the Sister thing was still in my head. It just wouldn't leave me. It had been there in my head all through grade school. I remember from a very young age always having a desire to be a Sister. And then when men came into my life, I sort of dropped that thought, but it came to the point where I knew I had to make a decision. I chose the Sisterhood.

I had my sweetheart take me to the train, and I never told him I was entering the convent. All he knew was that I was going to St. Paul, Minnesota. And so I went to St. Paul and spent a few days at a convent. One day I was talking with a Sister and somehow I said, 'I want to be a Sister.' And she said, 'Well, you can be a Sister in February or in August, but I would rather that you wait until August.' I said, 'Oh, no. I have to be a Sister as soon as I can.'

On the second of February 1948, I entered the convent. Well, February 14, Valentine's Day came and I hadn't told my little sweetheart that I had entered the convent. So I got a nice letter and a box of chocolate candy from him in the mail. Our Superiors could open our mail, so my Superior said, 'By the way, Margaret, I want to talk to you. I think you need to make up your mind about what you really want.' She said, 'If you want to go home with your sweetheart you certainly can, but if you want to stay, you stay.' I said, 'Well, I want to stay in this convent.' So I had to write him and say, 'Sorry, sweetheart, but goodbye.'

I am forever grateful for the choice I made. How faithful Jesus has been to me! He really takes care of all my needs and not only that, He even anticipates all my needs. Daily I ask that I be faithful to Him to the end of my life. As I reflect on my life, I can see the great love and plan He had for my life."

And thus ended the life of Margaret Gefre and thus began the life of Sister Rosalind.

### FROM A LIFE OF LACK TO A LIFE OF "LUXURY"

The contrast of living on a farm in North Dakota and living in a city and place with modern conveniences such as electricity, running water, showers and toilets, was dramatic to Sister Rosalind. This is what Sister Rosalind had to say about her impressions upon entering the convent in 1948.

➤ "I thought the Sisters were so rich. Here I come from the farm where there is absolutely nothing. Then I entered a convent, and I didn't even have to change clothing every day for different tasks. At home on the farm, I had to change my clothes to milking clothes, working clothes and then sitting-around clothes. And at home we had kerosene lamps. Every night we had to fill the kerosene lamp, and then would have to wash the kerosene chimney, and that was really lots of work for us kids. But when I entered the convent I would just flip a switch and there was light, and there were showers, even hot water, and I thought these were the richest people in the world because they had electricity, they had water, and I could bathe. It was like a totally different world for me.

When I was on the farm, we had absolutely no books at home except what we read at school. These books never belonged to us. They were school property. The convent had a room full of books and, above all, they had the lives of the saints. What a blessing these books were. I was so hungry for God and these books helped me feed that hunger. Even now, the Bible and lives of the saints still feed my spirit.

I missed speaking German and there was only one Sister in the Convent who could speak German with me. She was so very good to me. And it was hard for me to be in a place with all the trees around. I felt closed in. At home there were no trees, and I could see the sky all day long and the stars at night. In fact, I still miss the open prairie, and the beautiful clouds, and the huge rainbows after the rain. And in the very cold winter mornings we would see what we called 'three suns.' I have learned that people call them 'sun dogs.' Whatever they are called, they were so beautiful."

*Chapter 6*

# Surrender, Service, and Sacrifice

*"Well, life in the convent was not good for me." (crying)*

TWELVE DAYS AFTER Sister Rosalind entered the convent, she attended a Valentine's party put on by her religious community:

➤ "A friend had given me a beautiful red apron with a heart and covered with ricrac and I wore this fancy apron. I was so proud of it. My Superior came along and she said, right then and there, 'You know, you ought to be ashamed because this is the feast of St. Valentine and he is a martyr and here you are wearing this apron.' I couldn't see the connection, and I was so put down. I felt so humiliated and my evening was ruined. And I encountered that a lot living in the convent. It seemed that no matter what I did I was wrong.

I would go to classes with the group I started the path of Sisterhood with. The classes were taught by an instructor. However, my Superior would come and say, 'Why are you in this class?' And I would say, 'Well, this is my class, this is where I need to be.' Then she would say to me, 'Go down to the kitchen and wash dishes. Go and help them down there.' So I would go down. And the Sisters in the kitchen would say, 'No, we don't need you so you just go back to your class.' During the summer I would be sent out to weed the garden which was okay with me because

I always liked gardening, but I always felt that I should be with my group in those classes. In the winter again I was sent to the kitchen and they usually didn't need me there. Sisters in the kitchen would say, 'Go back to your class,' and I'd go back and say, 'Well, they don't need me,' and then my Superior would say, 'Well, then go out and shovel snow, and off I would go to shovel snow.'

And so I was always sent from one thing to another, and I felt it was because I spoke German and didn't speak good English, and they were ashamed that I wasn't educated. I felt I was kept from classes because I wasn't an educated person. I always felt, no matter what I was doing, that I was sent someplace else to do something that was lower, humanly speaking. Of course, in God's sight there is nothing low. And I knew God had called me. And I know God was very good to me there. So I stayed because of that calling.

I kept wanting to leave the convent because of how I was treated, but the call to the Sisterhood was so strong I just could not leave. I wanted so much to be trusted and loved. I felt loved by the Sisters but Superiors seemed to find fault with me almost constantly. I remember when I was told I couldn't even put vegetables properly on plates. I felt so demeaned."

Life in the convent was tough for Sister Rosalind. She found herself having to serve in a way that was least desirable for her.

"I did cooking for many, many years for the Sisters, and I really hated it. I hated every day of cooking, but I was asked to do it, so I did it. I did tell the Superiors that I would scrub floors or paint walls or do laundry, anything instead of cooking. So, of course, what did I have to do but cook for almost 20 years.

However, Jesus was very good to me. There were days when I thought I couldn't go on, but Jesus comforted me many times so I could go on another day. Of course, I could pray while I was cooking so that was a blessing to me. Many of the Sisters were very good to me and helped me especially with the dishes after meals.

I stayed because I took a vow to serve God as a Sister. And I took that vow very seriously. I was not just going to walk out because convent life was tough for me. I was going to stay and serve God."

Sister Rosalind sees God's purpose in the suffering she endured.

➤ "I look back and I really feel God was training me because I didn't know where else to go, so I always went to Jesus. I just believed that it was good for me. I would never not want to have gone through it because God strengthened me for all the other things that were going to follow. I learned to know that the only help I can get from any kind of place is from Jesus. So it was good for me to feel so alone."

And, finally, Sister Rosalind got to move on in her life and service.

➤ "My relief finally came. After 18 or 20 years, they finally took me out of cooking. I did dining room work at a hospital for a year, maybe two years, and I didn't mind that because my mind was free so I could still pray no matter what work I was doing. But I always had Superior problems. I don't really know why. I never did enough work for them. Here's an example: I loved concerts and one day the doctors had donated tickets to a concert for all the Sisters I worked with, but we all had to go to the Superior and ask if we could go. So all the Sisters asked and they were all given permission to go to the concert. But when I asked for permission, I was told, 'No, you cannot go.' And the Superior told me the reason I could not go is because I had to learn to work and obey. And I really feel that I was very obedient. I worked very hard, 12 to 14 hours a day in that dining room, but yet I was told 'You cannot go because you have to learn how to work.' Yet all the other Sisters could go. That's sort of how my whole life has been. I was not allowed to do what others were allowed to do. I was not allowed to go to school even though I wanted more education. I especially liked theology, but I was never allowed to study because they always needed me to cook. It would just have filled my heart to learn more about God. But I had to stay home and do the cooking. So I read a lot, and I guess Jesus loved me and taught me a lot through all these experiences. This was my only comfort, feeling so loved by the Lord."

Sister Rosalind was also subjected to psychological testing.

➤ "I was put through psychological testing. I have no idea how the testing came out. I was told by one of the Sisters that I was not bright, that I was unable to learn. And she said, 'We can't send you off to any education because your gifts are to work with the old Sisters.' Well, I didn't believe that. The real reason was that we had a home for our aged and retired Sisters and it was believed I could fill in and do aide work there. I love the older Sisters very much but I did not want to spend a lifetime working with them. But I was told that I was not sharp enough to go on in my education, so I was sent to our home for our aged and retired Sisters.

I worked as a nurse's aide at this home. My attitude was that I would go wherever God sent me. I remember that I was still quite young at that point, maybe in my late 30s, early 40s. I was always put on schedule from two in the afternoon until 11 at night, so this meant that I had no young life, being able to do what young people do at that age. Then one day I asked about working different shifts and my supervisor told me that I was just a young snip and I needed to learn to obey. Although I continued as a nurse's aide, at the same time I was thinking of going into nursing. So, on one of my free days I went and took an entrance test in Hastings, Minnesota, where the nursing school was located. I passed the entrance test, and the acceptance letter for attending nursing school arrived at the convent.

Of course, Superiors could rightly open your mail, and so my Superior brought me the letter and said, 'What's this about?' And I said, 'I'm going to nursing school.' I took this entrance test for nursing and I passed.' This did not go over well at all. One Sister tried to block this, but my higher Superior told me she would let me go.

When I left to go to school and said goodbye to my immediate Superior, she said, 'Oh, you don't need to say goodbye to me. You're too dumb, you'll never make it, and you will be back pretty soon.' I remember as I walked out I was weeping in my heart. I had expected a happy remark instead of being told I was too dumb.

I went to nursing school and I did well with nursing except for numbers. I was not good with numbers because they have absolutely no meaning to me, and so in all my classes I did well except for pharmacology. All my grades were good except pharmacology. I got terrible grades with pharmacology, so I thought, 'Lord, I have to leave school and go back to my old life in the kitchen.' So I wrote a letter to express my intention to leave school. But there was another Sister in my class who was very good to me, and I showed her the letter that I had written, which I think took me a week to write because I am not good in spelling or putting letters together. I wanted it to be a good letter, and I showed it to her and she said, 'You take that letter and tear it up. You're not leaving because all your other grades are good and that's going to pull up your lower grades.' And so I stayed and I passed with flying colors. From then on life changed for me, and what a wonderful change it was. It has never been the same. It was a wonderful change."

*Chapter 7*

# Nursing, Family Duty and a Miraculous Healing

*"My whole life changed when I got into nursing."*

C ATHOLIC NUNS formed the backbone of the nursing and teaching professions throughout the 19th century. When Margaret Gefre considered entering the convent in 1948, nuns were still very active in teaching and nursing. Nursing was a natural path of service for Sister Rosalind to take. She never imagined it would take 20 years to get a break. At that point, she got the opportunity to go to nursing school to become a Licensed Practical Nurse (LPN). She doubted her ability to succeed and planned to drop out, but a Sister who was in nursing school with her encouraged her. Through this encouragement, Sister Rosalind decided to stay in school, became a nurse, and permanently changed the course of her life.

➤ "My whole life changed when I got into nursing. I mean, it just changed. I couldn't wait to get up in the morning and to get to work. Even off days were hard for me because I wanted to be at work. On off days I would observe surgeries so I could better care for patients after surgery. So that's when my life really changed, when I got into nursing. I loved it. I was sent to Fargo, North Dakota, since I asked to go to a small place because I wanted to have my hands in everything and I wanted to learn more. And I loved it there.

Then one day Sister Rosalind came home to the convent in Fargo from a retreat and there were letters and telephone messages calling her home to take care of her mother, who was dying.

➥ "My mother had complications from a variety of things. I thought she'd be dead in about a week. Instead she lived for three years. I lived with her for those three years, taking care of her. I am forever grateful to my Superiors who allowed me to stay with her until she died. I was the first of the Sisters in my community to be allowed to stay with her sick mother."

It was during this time that Sister Rosalind was going to have a life-altering experience that would take her yet in a new life direction.

➥ "One day my mother said to me, 'There's a woman who lives down the road who does massage. You take me over there for massage.' So I took my mom to see her and she had a massage. And I saw a flyer there about foot reflexology. Foot reflexology wasn't well known at that time, but I picked up the flyer and I asked the massage therapist if this was anything worthwhile and she said, 'Oh, yeah, yeah, you go to the workshop and when you come back you and I can practice foot massage.' So I went to a weekend workshop on foot reflexology and I came back and called the therapist and asked if I could meet with her to practice foot reflexology. And she said, 'Oh, let's not practice reflexology tonight. Instead, I'll give you a massage.'

Before I knew it, I was on the table and had a massage. Up to that time I had been having chest pain for years that I always felt I'd die of because of night after night, when I went to bed I had to get up and walk around or sit up in bed because that chest pain was there continually.

The days were not bad, but the nights were very painful. And then the massage therapist gave me a massage, and I didn't say anything to her about my chest pain, and I didn't think I should even mention it. I felt if doctors couldn't help how could she?

I'll never forget that first massage. I felt light and free as a bird. I felt I could raise my arms and fly. I had ridden a bicycle, so I had to ride it home. Otherwise, I think I would have been able to fly.

That was the end of my pain, which I had experienced for 20 years. It just disappeared and that's why I started looking for a massage school. Every year before this massage, I had spent between one to two weeks in the hospital with doctors trying to diagnose the cause of my chest pain. Yet no one could diagnose or relieve me of this pain. I have no idea why the pain disappeared, but it has been gone ever since that first massage and has never returned.

After this remarkable healing experience, I immediately knew that God was calling me to practice massage, and I began to search out how I could learn it. I couldn't leave my mother to go to school, so I searched and searched to find a way I could study at home while caring for her. I found a 600-hour correspondence course, which taught a lot of anatomy and showed step-by-step, how to do massage. I was told about a blind gentleman in town who had studied Swedish massage in Chicago years before, and I ended up studying with him. In fact, he said, 'Anytime you need a massage, I will give you one so you can continue taking care of your mother.' My mom had both legs amputated and I used to carry her around and lift her in and out of a wheel chair, so I was experiencing some physical strain.

Of course, I still considered myself a nurse and I think I assumed I would continue with nursing, which I loved. But it was as if God made me understand that nursing was no longer for me and that I needed to go on into massage.

I learned massage through home schooling, and I graduated with flying colors. When I was with Mom I would sometimes massage friends in the home, not too many, just a few friends here and there, and I charged a whole $5 for an hour. And I worked at the Family YMCA for a little while in Aberdeen, South Dakota, where my mom lived. Taking care of her kept me very busy since by now she was completely helpless and required almost 24 hours a day care. I am forever grateful I had this opportunity. Since I had left home when I was still rather young, I really hadn't known her that well. In my youth, I thought that I knew more than my mom did. When I moved home to take care of her, I was amazed what a wise mother I had, and I believe she knew much more than I did. That was really a wake up call for me."

Sister Rosalind now had the training and experience to move into the next stage of her life, a stage that would take her into her life's mission: healing touch.

⤙

## Chapter 8

# The Path of Healing Touch

*"I felt I could no longer go back into nursing
and that was frightening to me."*

W HAT SISTER ROSALIND HAD EXPECTED to be a matter
of weeks of taking care of her mother had turned into
three years. Her mother suffered greatly during this period. While
taking care of her mother, a whole new world opened to Sister
Rosalind: the world of massage and healing touch. Her own healing
of long-standing chronic chest pain through massage had opened
Sister Rosalind's eyes to the value and potential of massage for
healthcare treatment for people.

"I directly experienced my own healing through massage.
This inspired me to take massage classes. Although I had
been a nurse, and I loved nursing, I was starting to feel
that I could no longer go back into nursing and that was
frightening to me. I was scared and several times I called a
dear friend in Fargo and told her I didn't know what was
happening to me. I told her I felt I couldn't do nursing
anymore. She would say, 'Well, you don't know what the
future holds, but you know Who holds the future, and
you must just trust in God.' And so I put my trust in God.
And my trust in God is what kept me going. I felt a call
inside of me to be involved in massage."

During this time of taking care of her mother in South Dakota,
Sister Rosalind began doing a little massage at the local YMCA and

in her mother's home. Then she had an experience that broadened the focus of her massage work.

➤ "You see, my first thing was to help people get rid of their headaches and backaches. It was so simple. Ten, fifteen minutes of massage and the headaches and backaches could be relieved. And then there was a strange little incident that happened. When I was still in Aberdeen, I did a few massages at the Y when Mom was well enough to spend a few hours alone. If she was too sick, I would give some massage in my mom's home.

One day when I was working at the Y, a woman came along and asked me what I did. Since I was brand new in massage, I said, 'Oh, I'm massaging.' And she said to me, 'Oh, you are doing healing just like Jesus did.' And I said, 'Oh, no, no. No, I am just massaging.' And then she repeated the same statement three times and I said, 'No.' And finally, afterwards I started to think, and I said to myself, 'You know, that really is what Jesus did. He touched people, He loved them and people would be healed.' And so, I then started to realize the real significance of touch, and my focus shifted to the importance of healing touch in people's lives."

When her mother died, Sister Rosalind returned to the convent in Fargo and spoke with her Superior about doing massage. Her Superior agreed to allow her to practice massage with the condition that it had to be done at a "reputable" place. The hospital in Fargo, where she had previously worked as a nurse, did not want her to do massage. They wanted her to continue as a nurse. This was the 1970s, a time when massage was not accepted and not practiced in most healthcare facilities. Since she had been allowed to practice massage at the Family YMCA in Aberdeen, she approached the Family YMCA in Fargo as a possible place for her to do massage.

➤ "I had no idea of what to do. I had always been assigned my jobs by the community, and I didn't know how to go out in public to find work. The other Sisters were saying to me, 'Why don't you stay with what you are—a nurse?' Nursing was nice, and in their eyes, massage was definitely not nice, but I knew it was a pure gift from God for healing. I knew I felt God's call, and I had to keep pursuing it. When I called the Fargo YMCA, hoping they might need a massage therapist, I was told they already had someone. As I contemplated what to do next, I began hearing a voice inside me saying very insistently, 'Call the Y.'

'Call the Y,' I thought, 'That's crazy, I've already tried that.' The words only got louder until I felt as if they were almost screaming in my mind. Finally, just to quiet them, I called the YMCA. The person who answered the phone that time responded to my question with 'Yes! When can you start?' I said, 'Right now.' And I started immediately."

Sister Rosalind ended up working at the Fargo Family YMCA for eight years.

➤ "At first I only massaged women. Then, after a while, the Y made arrangements for both men and women, and the women started bringing in their husbands and friends. When I began, I had to do massage in the exercise room, which was divided by several sheets draped as a curtain. When clients would share emotions and experiences, everyone in the exercise room could hear them. It just wasn't appropriate. As time went on, the Y recognized that this was a valuable service to their members, and assigned three rooms to me for massage. I hired another therapist and ran the massage program for eight years."

Practicing massage at the Fargo Family YMCA was a wonderful time in Sister Rosalind's life. She loved doing massage and was happy in her work and happy in her community. She felt that this was truly her calling and this work gave her immense joy and fulfillment. And she would probably still be there today if God had not moved her towards a bigger destiny. She was notified that her Superiors wanted her to return to St. Paul.

⤙ "Fargo had become home for me. My work was there and of course, my friends were there. I had been working at the Fargo Family Y for eight years when I got word from my religious superiors that I was to transfer to St. Paul, Minnesota. I really did not want to go. I cried a great deal and prayed and prayed. But, of course, I accepted. I've always believed that whatever happens, the Good Lord is in charge.

When I arrived in St. Paul, my Superiors didn't seem to know what to do with me. It was so difficult for them to understand how a Sister could do massage. For many people at the time, massage seemed to be associated with the 'red light district.' Of course, prostitutes were using 'massage parlors' as a front. So doing any form of massage seemed to connect me with that image in their eyes. I was determined to change that image. I had no idea of how to go about doing it, but, as always, the Lord opened the door. All I needed to do was walk through it. As I look back, I'm grateful for television, radio and newspapers in helping to make massage public."

Sister Rosalind was obedient and left a place and profession that she loved. She had to walk away from a life in which she felt happy, fulfilled and totally on course with the direction of her life. Leaving Fargo was very difficult for her, and after she was transferred to St. Paul, she made an attempt to leave the convent.

⤙ "I sent a letter to my Superior informing her of my intent to leave the convent, but I forgot to sign it. Since it was not signed, it was not binding, and I think she would have been glad for me to leave since massage would then have no longer been a problem for her to deal with. Several of my Sister friends asked me not to leave the convent, and they said, 'We have room for you.' I am forever grateful for their support and I stayed."

Even though Sister Rosalind wanted to leave the convent many times, she felt deeply bound by her commitment to Jesus:

➤ "I have many times wanted to leave the convent. The convent life has not been the easiest for me. But I made a commitment to the Lord Jesus Christ. He's my spouse. I'm His bride. He's my bridegroom. I just could not walk away in spite of the storms."

Because massage was not accepted in her religious community, the convent had to find something else for her to do. At first, they had her sit around. Then they sent her to work at the home for aged and retired Sisters. There she was, back in a kitchen, doing what she least liked to do—cooking food! However, at the same time she was doing massage for a few of the Sisters who wanted it.

➤ "Well, I went back to the kitchen preparing food for the old and retired Sisters. Basically I washed potatoes and carrots most of the time. Although I again believed that God's hand was in it, it was the last thing I wanted in all my life, and it was a very dark time for me. A few Sisters believed in massage, so on my free time at lunch or after work, I would massage them. And they loved it. It was a joy for me seeing Sisters slowly accepting massage."

Sister Rosalind continued in the manner until a new opportunity arose. She heard about the plans for her community to open Ascension Place, a center in the Twin Cities for women who were battered and who had drug, emotional and other problems. She really wanted to get out of the kitchen so she requested to work there. This request was accepted, and for two years she lived and worked at Ascension Place.

⟶ "I was at Ascension Place for two years, and that's how I got out of kitchen work. While I was at Ascension Place, I felt that those women needed prayer. You can do all the counseling and everything else, but if you don't get people to walk with the Lord or to pray, they can't be helped. So I would sometimes pray with these women because they came to me and wanted to talk about their problems, and I would suggest that we pray. I never forced my religious convictions on people, and they'd say, 'Yeah, we can pray.' So we prayed. Some of the other Sisters working there had found out that I was praying with these women. I was told that I had to quit praying with these women, that this was the last thing that they needed. I thought, 'Gosh, what a waste of my life if I can't do the most important thing in life, which is to pray with people.' So I resigned from there, and I moved to another convent.

At this time, there was a change in my Superiors, and I got permission from my new Superior to practice massage. So I began searching around for a place where I could do massage. I found a place on Grand Avenue in St. Paul and got approval to practice massage there. I asked my religious community if they would pay my first month's rent, and even though many in my religious community were still opposed, my Superiors approved the payment. I think it was about $75 a month, and it was only one payment for the first month. And that's basically the only help I've ever had. So that's where I started my massage clinic."

⟝

*Chapter 9*

# Grand Avenue Massage Center: Headlines and Notoriety

*"The next morning the Sisters opened the newspaper and found the headline 'Nun's Massage Parlor Closed.' Well, this was the beginning of trouble."*

SISTER ROSALIND finally had approval from her Superior to do what she felt Jesus had called to, therapeutic massage. And she had a place, 758 Grand Avenue in St. Paul! And her religious community was paying the first month of rent! Things were looking up. She was excited. She was happy. She was eager to start her massage practice. It was 1983—a time when massage was still identified with prostitution—and so she was doing a very bold and daring thing. She was a Sister providing massage services to the public.

➤ "I found a little place with two rooms and an office. When I went to take the required state examination for my massage license, I found out that the city licensing department had a set of specific requirements for opening a massage business including fingerprints, a mug shot and a $475 fee. They also had regulations about what to wear, when to open and when to close. These were clearly meant for 'massage parlors,' and I was being classified in the same group! There was simply no way I was going to submit to that, so I just went ahead and opened my place without officially registering it. I had passed my city-licensing exam, and I figured that was enough for what I wanted to do. It was February 1983, and I put some advertisements in the neighborhood newspapers saying, 'If you'd like a gift for your sweetheart for Valentine's Day, give them a massage.'"

After two weeks, Sister Rosalind got a visit from the City of St. Paul Vice Squad. They told her they were closing her down. She had no idea what the Vice Squad was, and she just could not understand why they were closing her down. She told them that she was a Sister, that this was legitimate massage. She showed them a letter from the city, which she said allowed her to operate her massage center. But her center was still closed down. She was up against a brick wall again. After struggling with her religious community in order to do the work she felt called to, she had finally had a victory. Now she was meeting with the same opposition in the outside community!

➤ "I was open for two weeks when officials from the city appeared. When they asked to see my permit, I showed them my massage license. They said, 'That's not enough. You're closed.' My heart just sank. I had finally gotten the okay from my Superiors, and now I was shut down."

With her massage center shut down, Sister Rosalind went back to the convent, not knowing what to do.

➤ "I went home feeling so hurt that I didn't tell any of the Sisters. I didn't tell the Sisters for three days. I pretended I was going to work for three days, but went to the home of a friend. I cried all the time. One day, during this time, the St. Paul *Pioneer Press* contacted me. They were trying to find out more information about this massaging nun and I just said, 'You know, I really don't have time for you. I am on my way to a prayer meeting so goodbye.' And I hung up.

I had never dealt with the media before. It was 9:30 at night and I sat at the prayer meeting and cried through the whole thing. I thought, 'Gosh, that was really nasty of me to hang up on them, and who knows what they will do because I wasn't nice.' So I called them back and asked them about what they really wanted to know. They told me that they heard I was closed down. And they asked me why I wanted to do massage. I told them that it made a lot of sense to me, since before Jesus healed people He touched them. The next morning the Sisters opened the newspaper and found the headline, 'Nun's Massage Parlor Closed.' Well, this was the beginning of trouble."

In the meantime, Sister Rosalind had to go to court.

➤ "In court, the presiding judge said, 'I can't imagine a Sister being dragged here before me. But since you're here, I'll have to deal with you.' Thank God he understood what I was doing and told me to go open my massage center and in thirty days appear before another judge. He told me he was giving me a 30-day injunction. So I went back to work, but I felt so alone. I used to cry when I was doing massage. Clients would say, 'Sister, you've had that cold for so long,' and I would say, 'I don't know why it's not going away.' It was such a deep pain not to be accepted for what I knew I was called to do."

After 30 days, Sister Rosalind met with another judge. He said the same thing as the previous judge: "I can't believe a Sister is being dragged here, but since you are here I have to deal with you."

Sister Rosalind got a lawyer, but soon dismissed her lawyer because she knew she could handle City Hall by herself.

➤ "I started dealing with City Hall. I only used the lawyer once or maybe twice. It was beautiful how people at City Hall became very understanding with me. I think it was because I didn't go in and act as if I knew it all. I went in, I suppose you'd say, humbly, and I didn't pretend to know it all. Many massage therapists didn't do well with their cities because they had an attitude of knowing it all. I ended up helping to rewrite many city ordinances. A city official would call me and say, 'We've heard about you, and would you come and help us? We are looking at a city ordinance, and would you come and help us rewrite it?'"

While Sister Rosalind was fighting these legal battles, she was asked to leave her home.

⟶ "Although my Superior's assistant was quite nice to me at this time, the pressure became so great at the convent where I lived that I was told that I could not stay there any longer. I had to move out because some of the Sisters thought that because I was practicing massage I was a dirty old woman. These Sisters were very disturbed that I was doing massage, which they considered bad, and that I was living at the convent at the same time. There were times when I would sit down at a table to eat with other Sisters, and some of them would pick up their plates and walk away. I'd step into an elevator and I was pushed away.

I was told I would have to leave the convent. I was told it was unacceptable for me to be at the convent any longer. So I lost my home. I contacted several other convents to take me in, but none of them would take me. I knew they all had space. They just didn't want me.

Finally, desperate for a place to stay, I called one of my lay friends who had been very good to me. I had spoken in her church. She was a wonderful Protestant woman. And I said to her, 'Do you know anybody who is going away so I can house sit?' And she said, 'Oh, my heavens. We've been praying. We need someone because my husband works at the University and is being sent to France and we've got two refugees staying with us and we don't want to leave them alone. When can you come?' I told her I could come right away.

I moved out of the convent on March 19, the Feast of St. Joseph. My Superior had told me then this was the last day I could be at this convent and that I needed to get myself out that day. I had an old, broken-down, raggedy car that someone had given me. The car had been sitting out all winter long. It was really useless. I packed the car, and was ready to go, and it broke down. So I had to try to get someone to fix it. I went to five o'clock mass at the convent, and I was just crying my heart out. I left and moved in with that wonderful Protestant family that had offered me the house-sitting opportunity. Above all, what I found so painful was that March 19 is a special day in my religious community and it was the day I had to move out."

Meanwhile, the *Pioneer Press* headlines of a Sister practicing massage attracted national attention. The story was carried over the international press wires and appeared in newspapers in Hong Kong, Italy, Sweden, Ireland and elsewhere. Sister Rosalind was contacted by other media people. She was becoming well known. She developed name recognition and this created many new opportunities for her to fulfill her mission of promoting healing touch through massage. The publicity was instrumental to the growth of her massage schools and clinics.

⟶ "The press was very good to me. They presented massage in a new light and brought massage out of prostitution and put it in its rightful place. I was featured in the Minneapolis *Star Tribune* newspaper, on radio and on television throughout the world. In fact, some media people came here from New York and called me about eight times in three days. They wanted to get me on TV, and I refused because I was so emotionally drained and upset. Well, you can imagine how I felt being regarded as a dirty old woman. And I was dealing with so much, and so I totally refused. I was embarrassed about all this news about me. It seemed wherever I turned I was in the news."

Sister Rosalind became active in changing city ordinances for massage, serving on a committee to draft amendments to the City of St. Paul's sauna and massage parlor ordinance. In 1983, the same year that Sister Rosalind opened her first clinic, the St. Paul City Council passed an amendment that:

1. Repealed the fingerprint and photo requirements.
2. Lowered the license fee from $475 to $200.
3. Set more stringent requirements for training and professional experience to screen out those who would use a massage business for prostitution.
4. Expanded coverage to include physical-culture and health services clubs and salons and weight-reduction clubs and salons.
5. Excluded licensed hospitals, sanatoriums, rest homes, nursing homes, boarding care facilities, medical doctors, osteopaths, chiropractors, physical therapists and podiatrists.

Not only was Sister Rosalind successful in keeping her Grand Avenue massage center open, she soon opened two more massage centers in Minnesota, one on Lake Street in Minneapolis and one in Edina.

➤ "Eventually therapeutic massage took its rightful place. In addition to working with the St. Paul City Council to rewrite the local ordinances, I have been working to create uniform regulations statewide, so that massage therapy will not be subject to restricting ordinances in various locales."

After considerable time, Sister Rosalind went back to living in her religious community. She had never officially left her religious order, but the majority of those in her religious community were still uncomfortable with massage. They felt it was something unclean, something not very nice. She was still ostracized by many in her community. These are very tough memories for her and still bring her pain when she discusses them. She has memories of being persecuted and of being very alone and having to stand alone, both in the outside world and the inside world of her religious community. Sister Rosalind was truly going through her Dark Night of the Soul.

➤

*Chapter 10*

# The Dark Night of the Soul

*"In the journey of the soul to God it passes through a dark night."*

THROUGHOUT THE AGES, mystics have described a process known as the "Dark Night of the Soul," a process of transformation and mystical union with God. The Dark Night has been studied and discussed both in terms of religious and psychospiritual experience.

The phrase "Dark Night of the Soul" traces its origins to the writings of the Spanish poet and Roman Catholic mystic Saint John of the Cross (1542–1591). He explains that the soul must enter darkness, must experience emptiness and abandonment, to be made ready for real union with God.

The Dark Night is a very difficult time, a time in which one feels totally alone. There is great inner suffering. There is no comfort in the outer world. There are trials and tribulations. There may be friends around, but friends cannot stop the inner pain. They cannot relieve the pain. There is nowhere to turn, except to God. The Dark Night is about transformation, about surrender, about preparing the way for the mystical union with God. In psychological terms, it is a time of transformative psychological growth.

A true saint, a true mystic, seeks God first and foremost. All else falls away in the pursuit of union with God. There is a hunger in the soul for communion with God. There is an inner compelling force to embrace God, to know God, to be led by the voice of God, to walk the path of God. The saint, the mystic, may cry out to God, may feel cut off from God, but he or she continues to strive. He or she labors through the Dark Night and endures.

Those who endure and achieve union with God, according to Saint John of the Cross, "burn with sweetness." Speaking of the "steps of the mystic ladder of divine love," he states:

➤ "The ninth step of love makes the soul to burn with sweetness. This step is that of the perfect, who now burn sweetly in God. For this sweet and delectable ardour is caused in them by the Holy Spirit by reason of the union which they have with God. For this cause Saint Gregory says, concerning the Apostles, that when the Holy Spirit came upon them visibly they burned inwardly and sweetly through love."

Those who become acquainted with Sister Rosalind comment about her great sweetness of character. Unassuming, humble and beloved by so many people, Sister Rosalind endured many years of the Dark Night. She speaks of crying all the time when she gave massages during the early years of establishing her first massage center. She cried during community meetings of her religious community when she had her first massage center shut down. In 1983, she cried when she was asked to move out of the convent, which had been her beloved home.

➤ "During that time my massage center was closed down, it was so horrible. Our religious community would have community meetings. I used to sit in the corner and cry and even though people might have cared about me, they didn't tell me that they supported me. I sat there all these months and months and cried at every meeting, and there were only three people who really stood with me. And then one day a Sister came up totally unexpected, not a Sister who is a hugging type. She came over and she hugged me and she said, 'I want you to know that you mean a lot to me. And I admire you; in fact, the Sisters

are admiring you for what you've done.' That's the first I
ever heard a statement of any kind of support. And that's
when my healing started to happen for me."

Through the Dark Night, detachment and suffering lead to
purification and illumination of the soul. Purification opens the
soul to receive the light of God and to let go of its worldly attachments and its ego attachments. This process can create an intense
spiritual struggle, hopelessness and feelings of isolation. One does
not know when or if he or she will attain a mystical union with
God. Sister Rosalind went through this struggle.

Another painful ordeal for Sister Rosalind was being forced to
go to psychiatrists by her community. When Sister Rosalind dared
to step out on her own and forge an unconventional path as a massage therapist, she went through natural emotional responses to
the undue stress of being condemned and ostracized not only by
her religious community, but by the world as well. Sister Rosalind's
behavior was viewed by some in her community as a sign of illness. Sister Rosalind was persecuted much in the same way as her
Patron Saint Margaret Mary, who was called a lunatic by many in
her religious order.

➤ "There were four Sisters who sent me to psychiatrists
because they thought I was very sick. So I went to psychiatrists, and at first I cried my head off because I thought
it was so dumb, and I knew I didn't need psychiatry.
But after the second time the psychiatrists would say,
'Sister, you don't need to come back. You are not sick.
The situation you are living in will destroy you, but you
are not sick.' And so they said, 'Don't come and waste our
time and your money.'"

To this day the memories of her painful journey open old
wounds and bring tears to the eyes of Sister Rosalind. But Sister
Rosalind adheres to the guiding words of her Patron Saint Margaret Mary, given on her deathbed as she was receiving the Last

Sacrament: "I need nothing but God and to lose myself in the heart of Jesus." Every challenge and suffering that Sister Rosalind has experienced has driven her closer to the heart of her Savior. These words of her Patron Saint give wise counsel:

➤ "But above all preserve peace of heart. This is more valuable than any treasure. In order to preserve it there is nothing more useful than renouncing your own will and substituting for it the will of the divine heart. In this way His will can carry out for us whatever contributes to His glory, and we will be happy to be His subjects and to trust entirely in Him."

The parallel between the life of Sister Rosalind and the life of Margaret Mary is very pronounced. Saint Margaret Mary's experience of persecution by her community is explained as follows:

*"These extraordinary occurrences drew upon her the adverse criticism of the community. . . . but her obedience, her humility, and invariable charity towards those who persecuted her, finally prevailed, and her mission, accomplished in the crucible of suffering, was recognized even by those who had shown her the most bitter opposition."*
THE POCKET DICTIONARY OF SAINTS, JOHN J. DELANE

What is the reward for successfully passing through the Dark Night of the Soul? It is the profound joy of achieving union with God. It is the caterpillar turning into the butterfly. It is perfect union with God through love. The fruit of the union with God radiates through the presence of Sister Rosalind and draws people to her wherever she goes.

➤ "It was only faith that brought me through all this. I know that God created our bodies to function in health and that massage can help with that. I kept believing that Jesus really wanted me to practice massage and that He would lead me through it all. That's what gave me the strength to move on. Massage now no longer carries the stigma it once did, and sometimes I think that maybe God needed somebody the public could trust to bring about this acceptance—perhaps a Sister could do that better than a layperson. Whatever it is, I am just grateful that God has used me in this way. And what a blessing it is to have massage in its rightful place!"

*Chapter 11*

# Business Growing Pains

*"I have learned that I don't know business,*
*but I have been able to let go of any pretension about this*
*and bring people in who know what they are doing"*

B Y EARLY 2003, there were five Sister Rosalind Schools of Massage and six Sister Rosalind Massage Clinics located in Minnesota and North Dakota, with a total of 150 employees. Since the inception of the first Sister Rosalind School of Massage in 1984, there have been over 2,000 graduates from all of the Sister Rosalind Schools.

Sister Rosalind never wanted more than one room to practice massage. She had no desire or ambition to build a large operation. And, in fact, there was little growth in her operations between 1984 and 1994. Then, in just three years, she opened three more massage schools. The growth coincided with an overall increasing acceptance of massage, many satisfied customers and many individuals interested in practicing massage as a career.

From a three-room massage center in 1983 on Grand Avenue in St. Paul, Minnesota, Sister Rosalind emerged successful and victorious over attempts to 1) shut her down; 2) steal away her business; 3) file lawsuits against her; and 4) betray her. The greatest disappointment came from the betrayal of the trust she had put in several people along the way. Sister Rosalind recounts one experience in the early stages of her massage ministry in which two of her employees tried to get rid of her and take over her operation.

⟫ "Two of my employees, one of them an administrator and the other one a massage therapist who went to our school and did massage with us, went to my religious community and told them that I was very mentally sick, emotionally sick, and I needed hospitalization immediately. These two individuals said they would carry on the ministry for me and they were capable of handling the ministry without me.

After they had gone to my religious community, one of them came to me and told me what they had done and that I was going to be called by my Superior. Sure enough, a few days after that, my Superior called me and said she wanted to talk with me. I went and I had a little talk with her and she said, 'Well, these two beautiful individuals came to me and you need to resign because sometimes people give birth to something but then their time is up and somebody else needs to carry on.' The Superior told me I would need to resign and go to a mental institution.

I told my good friends about what was happening. They became furious and said, 'No, you are not sick.' I told them that I was going to leave my massage ministry and enter a contemplative community because I always wanted more time for prayer. This is what I had wanted to do for many years. And they said, 'You are not going.' So four or five of my friends went to my community and said, 'We want you to know we are here, that we have heard about Sister Rosalind and that she is going to resign and that she needs to go to the psychiatric ward. We want you to know that Sister Rosalind is not sick and we will work with her and support her.' And this is how the clinics and schools were saved. But when I was told to resign by my Superior, I had been ready to submit to this demand and to go to a psych ward. I never ended up in mental hospitals because all the doctors said I had no mental problems, only that I was under immense pressure."

It is important to keep in mind that Sister Rosalind does not view the Sister Rosalind Schools and Massage Clinics as a business. She regards them as her "Ministry of Massage."

➤ "The Lord has been so faithful. I see His care all the time even through hard times. I am a child of God and He takes care of me. I used to walk through the halls of the building where my old massage center was located, and I would silently claim the other rooms in the building for Jesus. Eventually, as the other businesses moved out of the building one by one, all the rooms were being used for massage by us."

Of course there are business considerations of running a nonprofit organization, but behind the business end of the organization is Sister Rosalind's total and absolute commitment to God's work, much like the life and ministry of Mother Teresa, from whom Sister Rosalind received a personal, hands-on blessing when she traveled to India to meet the great saint in 1998.

➤ "I guess I've learned that if God wants something, no matter what the problems, He's going to get through. Mother Teresa used to say she was only a pencil in God's hand. And I feel I am not necessarily a pencil, but I am being led by God to make this ministry of massage reach many people. I have learned that I don't know business, but I have been able to let go of any pretension about this and bring people in who know how to manage a business, people who are very capable. Without them, I could not have gone on. In the past I trusted everybody, and although many of them were disloyal I have also had some very loyal and wonderful people who are with me today and who have given so much to make the ministry the success it is today. Ultimately, it is God's work. He is just and faithful and will continue to grow and protect what He started through a farm girl from Strasburg, North Dakota."

# Affirmation and Self-Worth

*"I believe that it is my mission to affirm others through massage."*

P ERHAPS ONE OF THE GREATEST effects of healing touch is the feeling of affirmation that it brings to people. Sister Rosalind has had many experiences of the profound impact of affirmation through massage. Sister Rosalind takes to heart Jesus' teaching that whatever one does unto the least of his brethren, he has done unto Christ.

"A gentleman came to me for a massage. He was very filthy. His garments were those of a street person, a person who has no place to wash and shower. But he came in for a massage, so I massaged him, and while I was massaging him, I visualized Jesus, which I always do when I have someone on the table. As I was massaging him, I massaged his scalp, and I said, 'Oh, you've got such beautiful hair.' His hair was filthy dirty, but it was beautiful hair, really very beautiful, so I just told him he had beautiful hair and he said nobody ever told him that before. And then I came to massage his face and I said, 'Oh, you have such beautiful eyes,' and he said, 'Nobody ever told me I've got beautiful eyes,' and he broke down and he started to cry, and I said, 'Well, I can't miss those eyes.' I felt he needed to know that he had beautiful eyes and beautiful hair, and I don't remember anything else about the massage, but he came back the next week and he was washed, he was bathed, and his body was clean.

And I massaged him again. When he came back a third time, not only was his body clean, but he had totally clean clothing, and I believe it was only because I affirmed him. I like to affirm people because I think we all need affirming and if people do good work, they need to know it. I've seen positive responses again and again after affirming people. I like to tell them that they've got beautiful eyes or a beautiful body or whatever is beautiful and good about them. One day I told a young man and a young woman that they were beautiful. And both of them broke down and started to cry. They said nobody ever told them that they were beautiful. Both of them said they felt ugly. 'Well,' I said, 'I can't help it.' It's probably the first time they heard they were beautiful and were not ugly. I feel if someone knows they are beautiful, that something about them is beautiful, then they feel better about themselves. I mean a person is truly affirmed. And I like to do that. I feel that it is my mission, and with the hugging people get a better self-concept. I also do lots of praying for and with the people I massage."

Sister Rosalind has made it a practice to visualize Jesus in every person to whom she has provided nursing or massage care.

➤ "I remember when I was practicing nursing, there was a patient that I was assigned to. Your patients would be assigned to you when you came in for your shifts. And as I walked into that room, there was a man who had these big warts or bumps that were part of his skin. They were not runny, they were just skin, but I really didn't want to touch them. And I walked into that room, and I thought, Lord, I can't handle this. I just can't take care of that man.

He needed a bed bath that day, and when I got the water and I started uncovering him and bathing him, I thought, 'You know, Jesus, I have the hardest time giving You a bath today. You are so ugly, but I'll do it just because it's You.' And by the time the day was over, I came to accept him as another patient and I was grateful and realized that I had taken care of Jesus that day.

Years back, people with a handicap lived in hospitals. We had a patient who was so demanding and controlling that everything you had to do had to be done her way. There was absolutely no other way but her way. When nurses were assigned to her, they often called in sick so as not to care for her that day. My conscience never allowed me to call in sick as much as I wanted to do so. As I took care of her, I'd tell myself, 'What an awful Jesus You are, but I'll take care of You anyway.'"

Sister Rosalind's ministry of massage addresses a major problem in society today—the problem of the unaffirmed person. Unaffirmed people suffer from a lack of self-acceptance. Massage affirms people. Massage promotes self-acceptance. Dr. Carl Jung has stated that self-acceptance is foundational to psychological well-being:

> *"To accept oneself as one is may sound like a simple thing, but simple things are always the most difficult things to do. In actual life to be simple and straightforward is an art in itself requiring the greatest discipline, while the question of self-acceptance lies at the root of the moral problem and at the heart of a whole philosophy of life."*
>
> Dr. Carl Jung

Every person needs affirmation. And when a person is affirmed, then he or she can affirm others. In his book *Born Only Once*, Dr. Conrad Baars points out the important need for affirmation and self-worth.

*"But what if I should discover that the least of all brethren, the poorest of all beggars, the most insolent of all offenders, yes even the very enemy himself—that these live within me, that I myself stand in need of the alms of my own kindness, that I am to myself the enemy who is to be loved—what then? Then the whole Christian truth is turned upside down; then there is no longer any question of love and patience, then we say 'Raca' to the brother within us; then we condemn and rage against ourselves! For sure, we hide this attitude from the outside world, but this does not alter the fact that we refuse to receive the least among the lowly in ourselves with open arms. And if it had been Christ himself to appear within ourselves in such a contemptible form, we would have denied him a thousand times before the cock had crowed even once!"*

DR. CONRAD BAARS

Dr. Baars defines affirmation as "having one's goodness revealed to oneself by another." He says, "This means that in being affirmed we come to know, on the sense level as well as on the intellectual level, our own goodness. We come to possess in acts of sensory and intellectual cognition or knowing that we are good and worthwhile, valuable and lovable."

Healing touch provides the perfect opportunity to affirm another human being on the sense level. Just the mere willingness to perform massage on someone signifies affirmation of that person. Sister Rosalind states:

➤ "I really believe that a big reason massage is so effective is that it gives people a feeling of being loved and accepted. Some massage clients don't seem only interested in being massaged. They are also interested in having a chance to talk about their pain and their problems. I keep my hand on the client just to be present to that person if and when that client break downs and weeps. I allow them to cry and I say, 'Just cry. It's OK.' Sometimes they don't even know why they are weeping. That, in and of itself, is healing. At times I ask to pray with them. That often is very healing. I have also noticed that some people have trouble enjoying a massage and that is because we still have that funny idea that to feel good is wrong. I tell them to enjoy the massage. That also is a gift from God."

Sister Rosalind had her own experience of being affirmed, an experience that changed her forever.

➤ "I came to wholeness 40 years ago because someone told me I was beautiful. I was at a point in my life when I felt I had nothing to give anybody. Then someone I respected very much told me that I had a beautiful face, and that I was a good woman. I needed to hear that. That's what brought me into a greater relationship with God because I didn't always think I was beautiful.

I could never accept myself because I had a big nose and I thought I was fat and I had a funny accent and I was not educated. These were strikes in my own mind until this person pointed out all these good things to me, and now it doesn't make any difference anymore that I'm not educated and I'm not beautiful and I'm not whatever. I can't change myself because that's how the Lord made me, and if I don't accept myself, it's like hitting the Lord in the face and saying, 'You know, you did a bad job with me.' Instead I say, 'Thank You, Jesus, You love me whether I've got a big nose and brown eyes, and I love myself and I love You.' This is what I do to people. Because I was affirmed, I can affirm others. Of course, this affirmation has to come from the heart and has to be true. I know many people have grown through affirmation, and that's what I want to do for others, affirm them.

There are times when I say things that are hard for me. I see things that are wrong and sinful. I speak against it and voice my beliefs. This is not readily accepted, but I believe

Graduation from
Nursing School

This photo was taken
before Sister Rosalind
stopped wearing the
habit in the 1970s.

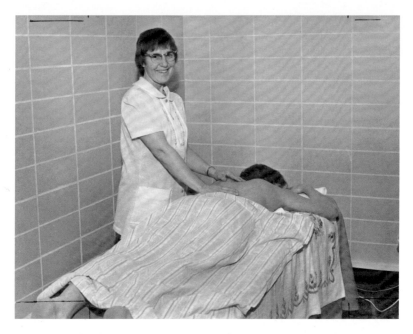

Sister Rosalind giving a massage at the Fargo YMCA, 1977

Healing touch

The strong hands of Sister Rosalind

Sister Rosalind has spoken to hundreds of groups

Highland Park
Massage Clinic

Sister Rosalind with actor and comedian Bill Murray

St. Paul Saints baseball game

Sister Rosalind and her students perform chair massage at all the
St. Paul Saints home baseball games

Sister Rosalind skydiving with a friend

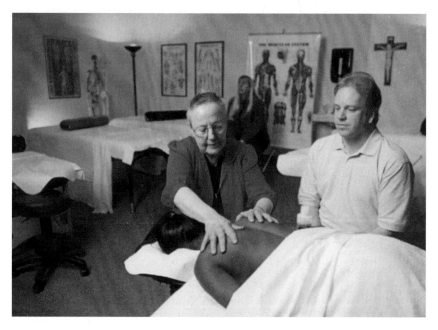

Sister Rosalind and Peter Fahnlander in West St. Paul campus
classroom, 2002

Sister Rosalind with Peter Fahnlander. Dedication of intentional healing prayer station at Sister Rosalind Massage School, West St. Paul campus

that it is important. If we follow God's laws, that frees us and we grow and are happier. Part of life is discipline."

Sister Rosalind learned much from her pain and suffering of not feeling affirmed, not feeling worthy, not feeling like a valuable person. She became very sensitive to other people and their need to be affirmed so that when she was affirmed she developed a desire to go out and heal others, just as she had been healed through being affirmed.

➤ "It seems to me that Superiors found fault with me no matter what I did. That always puzzled me. I really tried to be a good person. Faultfinding with me is changed now, but the effects are still there. At times, thinking of those days, I still break down and cry. Somehow that has never healed. I try not to blame my Superiors. It is just a fact. The other Sisters were very good to me until I got involved in massage. Many were not nice, but that too has changed, and now I feel much acceptance and love.

When I entered the convent, I was not an educated person. There were many Sisters who were highly educated, some of the highest educated women around, and I lived with them. I was cooking, which I felt was the lowest of the low. But I did it because I felt if my Superiors asked me to do something, to me it was God speaking to me, and so I cooked for almost 20 years, hating every day of it. Now God has brought me to where I am today. Again, what bothered me then was my lack of education. I had a strong desire for education in all areas, especially about God. It was hard for me to be deprived of education.

I finally took a GED test and I passed. So I got a high school degree. I went into nursing and managed that with flying colors. I went into massage and fulfilled the requirement of 1,000 hours to pass the North Dakota

state boards. I passed all of that. I am grateful for all this
education. I am aware how important education is, but
in no way do I look down on anyone who is uneducated.
They are many, humanly speaking, uneducated people,
for whatever reason, but what beautiful and gifted people
they are. I believe heaven is full of people who never saw
the inside of a school. It's who we are that matters."

Sister Rosalind states that people are "skin hungry."

⮕ "I remember when I first started massage. The big thing
was for me to massage away everybody's headaches and
backaches. I wanted to have them be healed from those
conditions. After a while I learned much more about
healing. One day a client came in and as I walked into the
room, she was crying and I hadn't touched her yet. I said,
'Would you like to share why you are crying?' And she
said, 'Because I'm so skin hungry.' I thought, 'My gosh,
here I am thinking I get rid of everybody's headaches and
backaches. Here's a woman who is so skin hungry, so
in need of touch.' And I started thinking about it, and
I thought about how so frequently before Jesus healed
people, He touched them."

Sister Rosalind believes that massage is not only a very powerful
tool to release stress, tension and anxiety, but it also makes people
feel valued and accepted and can bring them closer to God.

⮕ "People have no idea of what you can do during massage
to bring spiritual as well as physical healing. A client will
be on the table being massaged, and all of a sudden he
or she will break down and just sob his or her heart out.
Then because of who I am, I just simply enter in and say,
'Can I pray with you?'

And so I pray with them and I love them in the context of massage. I have experiences such as one woman who still stays in touch with me. She told me, 'I'll never forget when I came to you, I had cancer. I was sharing with you all my pain and what's going on, and you were so nice and you asked to pray with me.' That touched her. We are still friends. Every now and then she calls me and says, 'Come on, spend a night at my home.' So I go over to Wisconsin, spend a night with her and her husband. For me it's more about affirming, touching and just loving people where you can, just giving them a hug because hugs have tremendous power of healing in them.

I see when I hug people their eyes become alive and they say, 'Oh, wow, you mean I get a massage and I get a hug, too?' And I say, 'Oh, yeah. That's part of it.' When I was younger, I was called into the office and reprimanded because I hugged people and I talked with them. But I have always known the affirming, healing power of a hug and of touch. We see Mother Teresa almost always touching people. She knew the power of touch."

Research has proven not only the importance of tactile stimulation for affirmation, but also how touch can actually be a matter of life and death. During the 13th century in Germany, the emperor Fredrick II conducted an experiment with newborn babies. He had the babies taken from their parents and deprived them of any cuddling or verbal communication. He wanted to know what language these children would speak if they never heard any words. He did not find out because the babies died before they could speak. There have been many historical instances of children in orphanages being left alone in their cribs for months and years, and ending up being severely impaired or dying. Touch seems to be a basic human need, like food and shelter. Today there are many studies being conducted regarding touch and massage.

Sister Rosalind thinks that massage is simply one of the best medicines available in the world today.

➤ "I would like to see massage in every nursing home, hospital and every institution and especially in homes. Isn't that what Jesus did? He touched and people were healed. I think touch is so healing. People or children that have been physically or sexually abused often need massage for healing. I find both men and women are hungry for touch. Some never get touched at home. I have tried to provide places where people can get touched in a clean, reverent way."

➤

*Chapter 13*

# Spiritual Life and Experiences

*"I prayed to God for years so I could see Him in creation and God answered my prayer, and I saw Him in every leaf in the tree, every blade of grass, in all His creation."*

Sister Rosalind has been a natural contemplative, a natural mystic since childhood. A deeply spiritual child, she would become lost in communion with God when working in the fields or milking the cows. She meditated on God. She prayed silently when in the presence of others. Many days she spent the whole day just meditating on the Our Father prayer.

Devoted to God, Sister Rosalind has pursued an interior quest for God her whole life. She has had many mystical experiences with God. These are the fruit of her walking a path of sacrifice, service, surrender and selflessness and undergoing many purifications and testings of the spirit that have been both challenging and painful.

Sister Rosalind describes one of the turning points in her life when she received what she refers to as "the baptism in the Holy Spirit" and communion with the Holy Trinity. In Christianity, the Holy Trinity is defined as the union of the Father, Son and Holy Ghost in one Godhead.

"I didn't believe the Scripture when it said that God lives within us. The Bible does say that the Blessed Trinity lives within us. I didn't believe it because I couldn't understand it, but that changed for me overnight. I learned that it is true after I had a profound spiritual experience, which was a turning point in my life. Up to that time I was quiet and wishy-washy. After that I was a different person.

This turning point happened after I had been in the convent for several years. On one beautiful October evening, I was out walking with a Sister. I have no idea what we were talking about. I doubt that we were talking about God or Jesus because we usually did not share our inner walk with anybody, but I had a deep hunger. I know that.

As I was walking and talking, all of a sudden, like a flash, God simply made His presence known to me. I saw Him, I don't know how I saw Him, but I saw Him in every leaf in the tree, in every blade of grass. He was so around me that I could hardly stand it. When I say stand it, I mean literally. It was like a physical thing that took a hold of me. It was also a spiritual thing. I could not share that with the other Sister. She would have thought I was crazy and my Superiors would have put me in a psych ward. The experience was both painful and not painful.

The bell rang to go in for the night but God was so powerful that I was just completely taken by Him. We went in and said night prayer which lasted 15, maybe 20 minutes. After prayer, my experience continued. It would not leave me. And I quickly went up to my bedroom. All I could say over and over again, with the love of God pouring and pouring into me, was, 'My God, I love You, My God, I love You.' I had to keep telling God I loved Him because I was so filled, so poured full of His love for me. I remember falling on my bed and just continuing to say, 'My God, I love You,' and with that, I fell asleep.

The next morning I thought that was a really strange experience I had. I didn't know what had happened, but I knew that I was tremendously touched. My day went on as usual and I just kept wondering what had happened to me. At this point, I started reading Scripture. I couldn't put it down. Something had happened and I got a thirst for the Bible. A few nights afterwards, I had another experience. Always before I went to sleep I would pray that I would die young and become a saint and that if I died God would take me to heaven. At this time, I did not know Jesus personally. It was still God.

That night as I was praying the Blessed Trinity made His presence felt within me. It was just sheer delight. And then the words that it brought to my mind (and they are so imprinted on my mind that they can never be erased) were, 'If you love Me, you are going to be loved by My Father. We are going to come to you and make our home within you.' Those were the words. And I just simply enjoyed the Trinity. It was so heavenly. And again in the midst of this delight, the thing that stood out when the Blessed Trinity made His presence known was this tremendous gentleness. He was so gentle and He loved me so. That was all that I remembered at that point. Then I fell asleep.

The next morning when I woke up I thought this experience was really strange. I could no longer pray with my imagination. I mostly enjoyed just being in the presence of God, wordless. How I felt the Trinity taught me to pray was to enter within myself and just adore and love the Trinity. That was a real struggle because I kept trying to imagine Jesus or God or whatever about God.

This went on for two to three nights a week. I would just go to bed and pray as I usually did, and the Trinity would make His presence felt within me. But I didn't share it with anybody. At that point in my life, I needed somebody to direct me. I was frightened and yet I knew I was tremendously touched. Just two weeks before this, I tried to read the life of Teresa of Avila, who also had mystical experiences. I tried several times. I actually thought she was kind of in a world all of her own, and her experiences didn't make any sense to me. It just was not for me.

Well, after I had my own experience, I was seeking someone to help me. So I went to the library and I picked up the Teresa of Avila book again, and that is exactly what I needed. She became my guide. She kept saying that if any of these things happen to you, you should tell them to your confessor. So I told my confessor. I felt inside of me that he knew I was crazy and these experiences were probably from the devil. Anyway, I shared it with him and he said, 'You can have nothing to do with these things any longer.'

Even after I talked to my confessor, the Trinity would continue to come and I would say, 'Holy Trinity, You will just have to go. I don't have permission to be with You.' The Trinity did not literally go, and I refused to have anything to do with Him, but He stayed there very powerfully. This went on for weeks and months. It became very overpowering to have nothing to do with this, which I believed was the Blessed Trinity, but I obeyed. I went back to the confessor and I said, 'I just don't know what to do any longer because the Trinity is so powerful. He almost overpowers me. He just keeps coming back and letting me know how much He loves me.'

But my confessor told me I could have nothing to do with the Trinity. So I told the Blessed Trinity to go away.

Then some time later the confessor told me, 'Well, it's seemingly okay.' And after that I felt very free when the Trinity continued to come. I have no idea how long that went on, it might have been close to a year. At this point,

I gobbled and gobbled and gobbled Scripture and I also started to see how Trinitarian Scripture is, which I never did see before. Scripture and Teresa of Avila became my only books. Something had happened in my heart. I could no longer read the newspapers or other papers after that experience. Everything became so empty and painful except the Bible. That I just gobbled down. I was so hungry for God."

Then Sister Rosalind had another profound spiritual experience in which she and the Holy Trinity became completely and totally one.

➤ "One night as the Trinity made His Presence felt within me as usual, it was different from all the other nights I ever had experienced the Blessed Trinity. He started to make His Presence felt in my feet. He just moved up from my feet slowly all over my body, my whole being, my hands and my head. It felt like waves washing over my whole being.

Everything became covered with the Trinity. It was like I no longer lived and these were the words the Trinity gave me at that point, 'In Him we live and move and are and have our very being.' And the Trinity and I became totally and completely one. I was no longer me, and the Trinity was no longer separate. We were completely, totally one. I was lost in the oneness of God and I fell asleep.

The next morning my life was totally changed. Even when I moved my hands or my head, everything was so noisy, there was a desire for silence and more silence. It was like the whole world, even moving my hands, became so noisy. It was very, very painful. Not physically, but spiritually painful. I can't tell you what kind of pain. It was just a pain that I needed silence.

I felt a stronger and stronger need within me to enter within myself, just to worship and adore and love the Holy Trinity within me. By now I was a little more used to it because for many months the Trinity used to come in the evening. There was a total block in my imagination and I could not visualize Jesus, which was very painful for me. That went on for several months, so I had to learn to pray as God led me.

Then I started to say, 'You know, Holy Trinity, I know You really well now, but I don't know Jesus.' And I started to have a desire to know Jesus personally and I asked Him to let me know Him, too. No matter where I went, what I did, I would just close my eyes and the Trinity was right there. Prayer was so simple. Praying was as easy for me as breathing. These two just went hand in hand. I wanted both prayer and breathing. I couldn't live without either one."

Sister Rosalind had not been seeking these spiritual experiences. They came to her out of the blue. And these experiences created in her a deep love and adoration for the presence of God in the Sisters in her community.

➤ "What also started to happen with me after the Blessed Trinity became so present in my life was that I became more loving towards some Sisters I had a really hard time with. I had personality clashes with these Sisters. I had a hard time just loving them. And yet these Sisters did not know how I felt about them because they really loved me and were very nice to me. There were times when they came into the kitchen and I would have a human reaction of, 'I can't stand to have you here,' and on the other hand I almost fell on my knees in adoration of the presence of the Trinity within these Sisters. As long as the Trinity was within me, He was within these Sisters also.

And I knew that if I had fallen down on my knees literally, they would have thought I was simply crazy. I prevented my body from doing that, but in my spirit, in my heart, I literally went in adoration before these Sisters because of the power of the Blessed Trinity within them. I became so aware of the Trinity in other people. This gave me a greater love for every person.

Another thing that happened through these experiences is that I could pick up on the gentleness of people. If they were gentle people, that became powerfully, powerfully present. It was that same gentleness that I experienced in people that I experienced in the presence of the Holy Trinity. That happens spontaneously."

Sister Rosalind's great desire is to walk continually in the presence of God, and she has felt a great need for silence in her life ever since she had her spiritual experiences. At one point, she even requested to be transferred to a community where she could spend most of her time in silence. However, a priest counseled her that the world needed people like her to lead others to God, and she made the decision to be active in the world, for the love of God and the love of humanity.

"My community is an active contemplative community. As I think back even to my childhood, that is what I have really tried to live: to be active and contemplative, both at the same time. I was aiming at continually walking in the presence of God. This is still one of my great desires, to walk continually in the presence of the Lord, whether Jesus or God. The Lord is very, very present in my life.

After being immersed totally in the Trinity, that desire for silence never left me. It's still there, though not that strong. For years after that experience, I stayed with the community, but then I felt I needed more silence. I went to my provincial Superior at that point and I told her I felt there was not enough silence in my community and I needed to enter a contemplative community. She gave me the okay. I was excited about this. But as I walked out of the building a priest came along who knew me very well. I told him I was going to join a contemplative community and I shared with him why. And he said, 'The experience is genuine, but what if everybody who had these experiences ran and entered a contemplative community, who would bring people to God?' I said, 'I really don't know, but I need more silence.' He said, 'You stay where you are.' I am where I am because of that priest."

Sister Rosalind also has a very close personal relationship with Jesus Christ. She is devoted to Him, prays to Him, talks to Him and feels His presence.

✎ "One day, I was in the kitchen peeling potatoes and Jesus walked into the room. I felt Him like a person. He just walked in. He stood there and He was so loving and so gentle. I didn't see Him with my eyes, but I saw Him with my spiritual eyes, I suppose. And He just looked at me so lovingly. That was my first experience with Jesus. And then I had no further experience with Him until a few days afterward again. That time I was baking a cake. Again, He walked in and stood there so loving, so gentle. He seemed so pleased at what I was doing and then He walked out again. Those were two very special personal experiences with Jesus and now both Jesus and the Trinity are always present.

For instance, I sat in bed the other evening and I felt so much in the presence of Jesus. And I said, 'Oh, Jesus, I am just set on fire. I just want to love You so much. I just don't want to regret a moment when my moment comes to die. I just want to not regret any moment that I have wasted.' And I find that day after day after day, that's what I want

to do. In the real privacy of my heart. I continually tell
Jesus to set me on fire so I can love Him more."

Sister Rosalind describes how she communicates with Jesus.

━ "Before I go to sleep, we always have a little conversation,
Jesus and I. For me it's not a matter of saying lots of Our
Fathers and Hail Marys and whatever else. For me it's
talking to my friend so when I'm in my car, when I'm in
the garden, I just talk to Jesus. So it's like my friend with
me all the time, especially now that I live in the car as it
were because of all our schools and clinics, and I enjoy
that time a lot because I am never alone. I always take
Jesus with me. I tell Him that He can sit next to me.

I hear Jesus' voice inside, and it is so loving. I just feel so
loved and there are no words to it. You just know that
you are loved. You're just loved. And I think that's my
way of really communicating. Sometimes it's no words
at all. Sometimes I just am there and quiet and just love
Him and allow Him to be with me, and I just tell Him that
I love Him a lot.

I just love Him bunches. I talk to Him like I talk to a friend.
It's the most simple thing. You know how people say that
you have to have a technique. Well, I've never in my life
had a technique. When I was a little girl I'd be out in the
field, and also in my teenage years, when I was milking I
would either be singing Jesus songs or I would be praying, and I tried to pray the rosary while I was milking and
being out in the field, cleaning the barn, whatever. I could
never really use words. He was always a presence there.

I love to go to Mass because it is so wonderful to receive
Jesus in Holy Communion, and as I leave church I try to
carry on that communion during the day. I live in the
consciousness that we are His holy temple and that the

Blessed Trinity lives within me, and so I enter into this temple. And again I am just there. I talk to Jesus, the Trinity like they are my friends. I have no walls. And I think it probably happened as a child even though I didn't know God that well. But I know when I went to Mass, I could never use prayer books. I just had to kneel there in His presence. And that's still what I do very often. I just kneel there and I don't know how you would explain it, but I just allow myself to be loved."

When Sister Rosalind took her vows to become a Sister, she vowed to be the bride of Christ. To this day, she has the same commitment to Christ.

➳ "When I entered the convent, we could choose a name because entering into religious life, it's like a new baptism, it's like we start a new life, and I really looked at it as being baptized anew and starting life all over again. When we enter religious life, it's like getting married; in fact, we wore wedding gowns those days just like a bride. And when our names were changed, we exchanged our old names for our new names. To me it was like being married to Jesus Christ. He became my spouse. And that's how I still stand. In fact, people sometimes look at my ring and I say, 'Well, guess who I'm married to?' Or if they say, 'Ah, could I marry you so I can get a massage?' I tell them, 'Guess what? I am married to the King of Kings.' And I really believe that."

Sister Rosalind had developed a close relationship with the Holy Trinity and with Jesus, and then wanted to also know the Father. So she prayed to Jesus to reveal the Father to her.

➳ "Then I started praying, 'Jesus, I know You really well and I know the Holy Trinity really well, but I don't know Your Father.' I asked Jesus many times to show me His Father.

One day while I was massaging, and I felt Jesus standing beside me. I said, 'Jesus, show me Your Father.' And then when Jesus did that I was massaging. Finally, not with my ears, but inside of me, I heard Jesus say, 'Well, you've been wanting to know My Father and I'm going to show Him to you.' And then Jesus brought the Father and said, 'Here is My Father.' And the Father was Light. It was a very bright Light and I could not see the Light with my own eyes. But it was so bright around me that I used to think, 'How come people don't see that?'

One day as usual, Jesus came again and stood beside me and said, 'Here's the Father.' And Jesus left. For two weeks, I was bathed in this Light. That was the Father. Gradually the brightness of the Light disappeared. But the Father became more present to me and I got to know Him as well as Jesus. Sometimes when I was massaging, Jesus stood there. Sometimes the Father would be next to me. Their presence was always such a kindness and gentleness. Jesus is a person; the Father is a presence to me."

Sister Rosalind also wanted to personally know the Holy Spirit, but she says that she has not yet had an experience with the Holy Spirit.

➤ "So after this experience, I told Jesus, 'You know, Jesus, I know You really well, and I know the Father, but I don't know the Holy Spirit.' I can't say that I know the Holy Spirit as well as the Father and Son, but I know Him a little bit. I still ask Jesus to teach me who the Holy Spirit is. I believe one of these days Jesus will reveal more of the Holy Spirit to me."

The spiritual presence of Sister Rosalind is very strong and the people she massages often pick up on her special quality of peaceful serenity and communion with God.

➤ "One time I was massaging a woman and she said to me, 'When I come in for a massage with you, I enjoy it so much that I just want to be quiet. What I feel about you is that you spend lots of time in prayer.' And that was true. At that time in my life, I would usually go to bed at 11 P.M. and pray until 2:00 or 3:00 A.M. It was because the Trinity was so present; I simply could not go to sleep until He withdrew His presence. She also said, 'I feel when you massage it's like Jesus is standing beside you.' And I had never shared my experience with her, but what she said was true.

I have a tremendous desire for prayer. I can't watch movies or television that are not related to the Lord. If I look at a tree or a sunset, my whole being is immersed in God. When I look at a tree, I am in awe. God becomes so powerfully present."

There is no loneliness or feeling of lack in the life of Sister Rosalind. She lives totally in the light, totally in the consciousness of serving God, and totally in the presence of Jesus.

➤ "I am an inner person. Inside of me is where I get my strength. I'm not a lonely person. I think I could be alone forever. My only feeling is there are all those people who are hurting, and I wish I could reach out to them. It is not because of my loneliness but because I see all these hurting people so I need to be out there for them. I could put massage aside and the active community, but I have such a hunger to bring people to Jesus. That's why I'm out there. There's a pain within me that people don't know Jesus. Many of us live up in our heads. I know that many are seeking and sincere, but we are so up in our heads. I know there are so many lonely people, but I don't feel lonely. I feel so rich. I just pray, 'Jesus, bring these people to a deep walk with You.' I have such a hunger for that.

And I have a hunger for my own growth. I know I'm not at the end. One of my prayers is, 'Lord, make me a flame that I might become a fire, a fire to be consumed with the love for You.' And I ask that God would consume me. I say, 'Give me a heart that I might burn with love for You.' I have that desire. I am not there. In no way. In fact, I feel very far removed. I have this desire for a deeper and deeper walk with Jesus. And yet, even that desire has to come from Him. I know He's given me that desire even as a child. I still keep asking that I may become a saint. Now I ask that I might become a great one. 'Lord, make my heart a flame that I might become a pure love for Thee.'"

Sister Rosalind feels that there is no excuse for active people not to walk with God. She leads an extremely active life, spending much of her time with people. But her heart and mind are always seeking for God.

"I think that unless we have a deep spiritual life our actions are totally empty. I have very little time to pray alone. I am so involved with people. I am up at 6:30 A.M. in the morning. I go to Mass, I pray. Much of my praying is done when I go to work. My whole thing is to walk in the presence of the Lord. You should try 100, 1000 times a day, and if you fail, come back and try again. That's how I learned. As a child, I would say I never continually thought of God all day. It's a continual bringing ourselves back to God. I know that for me it is trial and error. Even now, I am not always walking in the presence of the Lord. There are times when I go half a day. I'm so involved with people. But I come back very gently and I do not condemn myself, I just know that the Lord will give me the gift. It is a gift to walk with Him."

Books have been written by and about the saints who have had mystical experiences with God. Many times the world just does not understand the life and experiences of a saint, the life of a mystic. Sister Rosalind did not even believe or understand until it started to happen to her.

There is no doubt that something special resides within Sister Rosalind. A regular attraction at the St. Paul Saints baseball games every year, people flock to her at games, events, her public speeches. People bask in the sunshine of her love, her warmth and her healing and affirming touch. Strangers approach her in parking lots, restaurants, on the street. They are excited and thrilled to see that special Sister who has brought so much good to so many lives.

If ever there was an exemplary spiritual life, it is the life of Sister Rosalind. She is real, humble, unpretentious, strong and persevering. She has made the pursuit of God the goal of her life, she has paid the price through sacrifice and service and she has reaped the rewards that come to the true servants of God.

～

*Chapter 14*

# Spiritual Healing through Christ

*"When you walk with the Lord,*
*you really put on the mind of Christ."*

T HE IMITATION OF CHRIST is tangible in the life and presence of Sister Rosalind. This tiny woman radiates a powerful presence that fills a whole room. When you meet her, she will give you a big, unreserved hug, right from the heart. If you receive a massage from her, you will be amazed at the strong, powerful hands on such a little woman.

Much of Sister Rosalind's time is spent giving speeches to organizations and businesses and giving massages to people in hospitals, nursing homes and in their own homes. A walk through her corporate office and flagship West St. Paul massage school reveals the spiritual foundation of her schools and clinics. There are crucifixes on the walls. There is a request book for prayer for people who need healing. A picture of Jesus walking across the water appears at the entrance of the school. A Sister acts as the school receptionist.

Sister Rosalind explains that the Sister Rosalind schools do not push religion:

"Our schools are not Catholic schools, but Christian schools. However, nobody has to change their faith to go to our schools. I don't push my religious convictions, but I do want people to be motivated to practice massage not just for money, but to serve other people. If we are faithful, God always provides. I find students choose our schools because they are good schools."

Sister Rosalind believes that healing truly comes through Christ, and that putting on the mind of Christ is important not only for the healer but also for the person who desires to be healed. She encourages people to actively seek to put on the mind of Christ.

"Walking with the Lord doesn't happen instantly. All my life it has been a part of me, but I have had to keep cultivating it. For me, it took years and years. The Lord keeps tugging at me if I don't take that time to walk with Him. There's a continual pull within me, that pull between solitude and the desire to be out there to bring people to the Lord. I pray every day that people will become spirit-filled. We do all this head stuff. It's like two different worlds: here's the world down here and there's the world up there.

I understand the world down here because I live here, but what I want to do is keep bringing people to the world up there where they see double vision. We are literally putting on Christ, putting on the mind of Christ. When we put on the mind of Christ, we can no longer think the way the world thinks. I no longer think the way the world thinks with thoughts like, 'You did this to me so therefore I'm going to do that to you.' My first thought that comes is to not return evil for evil, but to the contrary, to return a blessing. When we walk with the Lord, we really put on the mind of Christ."

Sister Rosalind says that oftentimes a person may receive a spiritual healing that does not necessarily manifest as a physical healing. She has seen people emotionally, mentally and spiritually transformed through healing touch.

Through personal contact, public appearances and the media,

the message and person of Sister Rosalind has reached millions of people far and wide throughout the world. The obedience to the call of God, the faithful commitment to God and the overcoming of many obstacles has revealed a giant of a woman. This little farm girl from Strasburg, North Dakota, uneducated and unsophisticated, has made a major impact in the establishment of healing touch as a respected and popular healing modality.

Some day when the tourists go to Strasburg, they will be going to visit the farmstead not only of Lawrence Welk, but also of that saintly woman and great pioneer of healing touch, Sister Rosalind Gefre. Her name will go down in history as one of those great trailblazing, self-sacrificing and courageous souls who gave their lives to make the world a better place for a suffering humanity.

# About Sister Rosalind

SISTER ROSALIND GEFRE (pronounced with a hard "g") was born in 1929 to the descendants of German immigrants who had a farm near Strasburg, North Dakota, the hometown of the famous television personality Lawrence Welk. Growing up, Sister Rosalind spoke German in her home and suffered the tragic loss of her father at the age of six. Perhaps a foreshadowing of her life to come as a Sister dedicated to healing was the selection by her parents of her birth name of Margaret. For her confirmation name, Sister Rosalind took Margaret Mary after a saint she dearly loved—Saint Margaret Mary Alacoque, who was born in France in 1647. As a child, Saint Margaret was confined to bed with paralysis for four years. After making a vow to the Blessed Virgin that she would consecrate herself to religious life, Saint Margaret was instantly healed.

In 1948, Sister Rosalind left North Dakota for the Twin Cities in Minnesota to enter a Catholic convent to become a Sister. She became a Licensed Practical Nurse in 1968 and was then assigned to Fargo, North Dakota. Her mother became terminally ill, and Sister Rosalind moved in with her mother in Aberdeen, South Dakota for three years to take care of her. Her mother wished to receive massage therapy to help with her pain, and Sister Rosalind took her to someone who ended up also giving Sister Rosalind a massage, which permanently healed her of a chronic chest pain that she had had for 20 years.

Amazed and impressed with the healing power of massage, Sister Rosalind began studying massage technique and then began practicing massage at the Family YMCA in Fargo in 1973 and continued there for a total of eight years.

Sister Rosalind was then assigned by her community to return to the Twin Cities and had several very challenging years of overcoming obstacles and opposition to her mission to bring healing to people through massage.

Eventually, Sister Rosalind opened her very first clinic in 1983 on Grand Avenue in St. Paul, Minnesota, and made headlines in the newspaper when the Vice Squad shut her down for not having a license. At that time, massage "parlors" were associated with prostitution, and Sister Rosalind was pioneering massage as a healing art. The founding of Sister Rosalind's first school came a year later in 1984. Now she has several massage schools and clinics in both Minnesota and North Dakota.

A regular attraction at the popular St. Paul Saints baseball games, she can be seen giving massages at every game. She has been featured on television, in newpapers and in magazines, and has given hundreds of speeches to groups. Sister Rosalind is known for her warmth, her caring and her expression of God's love through healing touch. Her schools and clinics are based upon Christian principles and their mission is to promote healing of the body, mind, and spirit through touch. Sister Rosalind believes that God created our bodies to function in health to achieve the fullness of life, and the schools and clinics seek to work in harmony with God's plan.

~

# Sister Rosalind Writings

S ISTER ROSALIND has always felt quite handicapped by her lack of education and her poor English skills because of being raised speaking German. Consequently, she has not created much written material, and it is very painstaking for her to write letters, speeches and articles. However, she has written some beautiful poems and some very articulate and expressive letters, which reveal her deep spiritual nature and her extraordinary life experiences.

## "DAWN"

### by Sister Rosalind

Dear Beloved Father Mine
I want to be completely Thine
And now at last the storm has passed
Let me rest secure within Thy hand.

I ponder what it all has meant
Oh, dear God will the storm return again?
Make me strong and hold my hand
That no one can hurt me again.

Life is so mysterious and strange
For none of us Your mind can read
Oh, my Father stretch out Your hand to me
So together Thy children to the kingdom we lead.

When all Thy children have reached their home
What celebration will there be around Thy throne?
Together with the Angels and Saints alone
We, too, will join in the song of love.
Amen.

## "TOUCHED"
### by Sister Rosalind

Oh my Jesus, Father, and God
I kneel before You completely dark
I'm stripped, naked, wounded and bruised
My Beloved Father and God I have nothing else to lose

How different Oh God are Your ways from mine—
It is from suffering, pain and shame that I run
Teach me Oh God I have nothing to lose
If I, like You, can humble myself.

Oh my Beloved Father and Son
Teach me Thy Spirit forever to want
That I may hunger to suffer like Thee.
That all who see me may experience Thee

Beloved Spirit may You always be praised
It is You who continually fill us with grace
May to the Trinity all Glory be sung
Forever and ever till Your Kingdom come.
Amen. Amen.

## "LOVED"

### *by Sister Rosalind*

Oh my beloved three in one
How long, how long will the storm run.
Teach me beloved to see only Thee
And so Thy heart my shelter be.

Oh my beloved the storm is so great
It seems I in the midst will be whirled away
Is it those whom I love You have sent my way?
That they be the ones to purify me.

Oh Beloved Father mine
Must my heart break before I'm completely Thine?
If this is the price You ask me to pay
Oh Father mine, I give it all today.

Take me completely Lord, no matter what the cost
I know that some day not far away
You in this temple purified and strong
Will whisper and say the victory is won.

## "REACH OUT"
### by Sister Rosalind

Help me Lord that I might say
All that is in my aching heart today
Bleeding, and wounded and hurt inside
Oh Divine Healer put Your hand into mine

Shall I ever again reach out in love?
Is it worth the risk to be cast aside?
Will You kind Father Thy love bestow
So all Thy healing may come to know

Help me Lord so strong I be
To reach out and touch no matter what consequence may be
Oh Lord heal me so a channel I be
To all who in pain will come to me.

## EXCERPT OF A LETTER FROM
## SISTER ROSALIND TO HER COMMUNITY

Fargo, North Dakota, June 23, 1980

Dear Sisters,

It has been over thirty years since I became a Sister in our community. All these years as a Sister in the service of Our Lord have been such a blessing to me. I cannot think of life in any other service than in serving Him. All of you are dear to me as we walk together as Sisters. Some of you are precious friends who have loved and nurtured me with your care and prayers for many years. Some things have been happening to me during the past few years that I cannot keep to myself any longer and need to tell each of you.

When I entered the convent I came to you with less worldly learning than most of you. I did not have a high school degree. You helped me improve my English. You let me serve you for several years in cooking. Then you blessed me by sending me to study to be a Licensed Practical Nurse. I got to serve Him as an LPN for awhile. Then my Mom's long terminal illness—three years—took me to her bedside for that time and I kept asking the Lord Jesus to give her peace during those last months. There were all the pills and injections the doctor could prescribe to try to bring that peace, the peace that He promises us. So I kept praying and praying. Sometimes I just talked to Him a whole day and all night asking Him to bring Mom peace in the few months she had left.

Something came to me. That peace of Jesus was to come to Mom through me! I could hardly accept that I could do anything more for her than I had learned to do with the LPN training, but Jesus kept telling me to keep listening to Him and He would lead me to be a channel for answering the prayer for peace for my Mom. And He did just that. I kept being led to His Word about love and about how He almost always touched people with His hands while healing them. Jesus led me by His Holy Spirit to start to pray with Mom first and then to lay hands on her and then to go from a nurse's backrub to a massage of her aching limbs as well. When I saw the peace coming to her I just started to rejoice that I could be used as a channel for peace. And that went on until training from a kindly massage therapist in town who taught me how to use my hands to help sprained ankles, pulled muscles, aching backs, headaches and so on.

After my mom's funeral I had to face the fact that a new ministry was opening for me. But how could I tell anyone about this ministry without getting strange looks?

There was an opening for a massage therapist at the Family Y in Fargo and I was able to get the needed permission to work there. That was six years ago. Now I have two nurses working with me as well as a doctor from South America who is still studying for his license to practice medicine here. We see many people each week. I am still often the one to see new people first. Sometimes after people have become well (and they usually don't get well without meeting the Lord personally as well as being touched and prayed with) they still come back to us but I usually refer them to others and spend more time with the ones whose bodies and spirits hurt the most.

Some things have happened here in Fargo to make me hopeful that my work is pleasing to my Heavenly Father—some people have just given me an open invitation to move my ministry into a House of Healing here. They would pay all the expenses and everything. Some have already given stationery and stamps and even a post office box. It is like some can't wait for all this to happen. But I do not have the needed permission and so will stay at the YMCA clinic while continuing to reside at the convent. My new friends in the Lord are also starting to pray with others for healing. It is such a blessing from the Heavenly Father to grow with others and to see them lead other of God's hurting children to wholeness, too!

Sincerely in Him,
Sister Rosalind Gefre

## SISTER ROSALIND PRAYER FOR HEALING

God Our Father we welcome You
and praise You here among us.

We thank You for Your Son Jesus.

It was Jesus who became man for us
So He could walk among us.

Thank You Jesus as You lived among us and saw
and bore our pain.

You had compassion on us
so You touched our sick and burdened bodies.

As Scripture says, "He was moved with compassion."

We ask that You walk among us, touch us, heal us.

Reach into the very depth of our hearts,
remove what is displeasing, our sins
for which You gave Your Life.

Forgive us and heal us however or wherever
we need Your healing.

We bring all our needs
before You and trust in Your goodness.

# About Saint Margaret Mary

I N HER CHILDHOOD, Sister Rosalind was profoundly impressed by the life of her patron saint. As it turned out, Sister Rosalind's own life took a similar direction, ending up with many mystical experiences and much success after years of persecution and opposition to her mission.

Margaret Mary Alacoque was born on July 22, 1647, at L'Hautecour in the province of Burgundy, France. As a child, she studied with the Poor Clares at Charolles. Her father died when she was eight years old, and she was bedridden from the age of 11 to 15. She joined the Order of Our Lady of the Visitation at Paray-le-Monial in 1671 and a few years later she was visited by Jesus, who asked her to spread devotion to his Sacred Heart. She did this only after she had received the permission and approbation of her Superiors. A chapel dedicated to the Sacred Heart was constructed at Paray-le-Monial in 1688, and the devotion to the Sacred Heart of Jesus began to spread. St. Margaret died on October 17, 1690, and Pope Clement XIII officially approved the devotion to the Sacred Heart in 1765. Pope Benedict XV canonized St. Margaret Mary Alacoque in 1920.

During childhood, Saint Margaret Mary was stricken with paralysis, which confined her to bed for four years. However, Saint Margaret Mary received instantaneous and permanent healing from this crippling disorder when she made a vow to become a Sister. In that instant, she was cured.

Saint Margaret Mary encountered tremendous opposition to her spiritual work.

*The Pocket Dictionary of Saints* by John J. Delane describes the life of Margaret Mary:

*". . . . in the cloister she chose for herself what was most repugnant to her nature, making her life one of inconceivable sufferings, which were often relieved or instantly cured by our Lord, Who acted as her Director, appeared to her frequently and conversed with her, confiding to her the mission to establish the devotion to His Sacred Heart. These extraordinary occurrences drew upon her the adverse criticism of the community, who treated her as a visionary, and her Superior commanded her to live the common life, but her obedience, her humility, and invariable charity towards those who persecuted her, finally prevailed, and her mission, accomplished in the crucible of suffering, was recognized even by those who had shown her the most bitter opposition.*

*Margaret Mary was inspired by Christ to establish the Holy Hour and to pray lying prostrate with her face to the ground from eleven till midnight on the eve of the first Friday of each month, to share in the mortal sadness Jesus endured when abandoned by His Apostles in His Agony, and to receive holy Communion on the first Friday of every month. In the first great revelation, He made known to her His ardent desire to be loved by men and His design of manifesting His Heart with all Its treasures of love and mercy, of sanctification and salvation. He appointed the Friday after the octave of the feast of Corpus Christi as the feast of the Sacred Heart; He called her 'the Beloved Disciple of the Sacred Heart,' and the heiress of all Its treasures. The love of the Sacred Heart was the fire, which consumed her, and devotion to the Sacred Heart is the refrain of all her writings. In her last illness she refused all alleviation, repeating frequently: 'What have I in heaven and what do desire on earth, but Thee alone, O my God,' and died pronouncing the Holy Name of Jesus.*

*The discussion of the mission and virtues of Margaret Mary contin-*
*ued for years. All her actions, her revelations, her spiritual maxims,*
*her teachings regarding the devotion to the Sacred Heart, of which*
*she was the chief exponent as well as the apostle, were subjected*
*to the most severe and minute examination, and finally the Sacred*
*Congregation of rites passed a favorable vote on the heroic virtues of*
*this servant of God. In March, 1824, Leo XII pronounced her Vener-*
*able, and on 18 September, 1864, Pius IX declared her Blessed.*
*Benedict XV canonized her in 1920. When her tomb was canonically*
*opened in July 1830, two instantaneous cures took place. Her body*
*rests under the altar in the chapel at Paray, and many striking fa-*
*vours have been obtained by pilgrims attracted thither from all parts*
*of the world. Her feast is celebrated on 17 October."*

During her life as a nun, Margaret Mary faced a great dilemma.
Would she obey her worldly Superiors and the rules of her Order,
or would she obey the will of God, which was communicated to her
during intimate conversation with Jesus in prayer? When she told
her Superior about her visions, she was treated contemptuously
and was forbidden to carry out any of the religious devotions that
had been requested of her in her visions. And she became ill from
the strain.

This conflict between obeying the will of Superiors or the
will of God is frequently seen in the lives of the saints. Margaret
Mary's Order persecuted her and tried to withdraw her from her
communion with God's voice. They threatened to send her away.
Many called her a lunatic.

Margaret Mary was sanctified by many trials, and Jesus appeared to her, showing His Sacred Heart. There are records of the
messages conveyed to her by Jesus. On the Feast of St. John, the
Beloved Apostle, December 27, 1673, Margaret Mary related that
on this day Jesus said to her:

*"My Divine Heart is so inflamed with love for men, and for you in*
*particular that, being unable any longer to contain within Itself the*

*flames of Its burning Charity, It must spread them abroad by your means and manifest Itself to them mankind in order to enrich them with the precious treasures which I reveal to you and which contain graces of sanctification and salvation necessary to withdraw them from the abyss of perdition. I have chosen you for the accomplishment of this great design."*

The second great revelation of the Sacred Heart occurred in 1674. Margaret Mary states:

*"On one occasion, while the Blessed Sacrament was exposed, feeling wholly withdrawn within myself by an extraordinary recollection of all my senses and powers, Jesus Christ, my sweet Master, presented Himself to me, all resplendent with glory, His Five Wounds shining like so many suns. Flames issued from every part of His sacred humanity, especially from His adorable breast, which resembled an open furnace and He disclosed to me His most loving and most amiable Heart, which was the living source of these flames.*

*It was then that He made known to me the ineffable marvels of His pure love and showed me to what excess He had loved men, from whom He received only ingratitude and contempt. 'I feel this more,' He said, 'than all that I suffered during my Passion. If only they would make me some return for my love, I would think but little of all I have done for them and would wish, were it possible, to suffer still more. But the sole return they make for all my eagerness to do them good is to reject me and treat me with coldness. Do you at least console me by supplying for their ingratitude, as far as you are able . . . In the first place you shall receive me in Holy Communion as often as obedience will permit you. You shall, moreover, receive Holy Communion on the First Friday of each month.'"*

Communicating with Margaret Mary, Jesus assigned her a formidable task. She was to establish devotion to the Sacred Heart of Jesus in the Catholic Church. This task she did complete after much persecution, false accusation, illness and suffering. When she lay dying and receiving the Last Sacrament, she said, "I need nothing but God, and to lose myself in the heart of Jesus."

## THE TWELVE PROMISES OF JESUS TO SAINT MARGARET MARY FOR THOSE DEVOTED TO HIS SACRED HEART:

1. I will give them all the graces necessary for their state of life.
2. I will establish peace in their families.
3. I will console them in all their troubles.
4. They shall find in My Heart an assured refuge during life and especially at the hour of their death.
5. I will pour abundant blessings on all their undertakings.
6. Sinners shall find in My Heart the source of an infinite ocean of mercy.
7. Tepid souls shall become fervent.
8. Fervent souls shall speedily rise to great perfection.
9. I will bless the homes where an image of My Heart shall be exposed and honored.
10. I will give to priests the power of touching the most hardened hearts.
11. Those who propagate this devotion shall have their names written in My Heart, never to be effaced.
12. The all-powerful love of My Heart will grant to all those who shall receive Communion on the First Friday of nine consecutive months the grace of final repentance; they shall not die under my displeasure, nor without receiving their Sacraments; My heart shall be their assured refuge at that last hour.

## FROM SAINT MARGARET MARY ALACOQUE'S VISION OF JESUS

*from a letter by Saint Margaret Mary Alacoque*

"Look at this Heart which has loved men so much, and yet men do not want to love Me in return. Through you My divine Heart wishes to spread its love everywhere on earth. The Sacred Heart of Christ is an inexhaustible fountain and its sole desire is to pour itself out into the hearts of the humble so as to free them and prepare them to lead lives according to his good pleasure.

From this divine heart three streams flow endlessly. The first is the stream of mercy for sinners; it pours into their hearts sentiments of contrition and repentance. The second is the stream of charity which helps all in need and especially aids those seeking perfection in order to find the means of surmounting their difficulties. From the third stream flow love and light for the benefit of his friends who have attained perfection; these he wishes to unit to himself so that they may share his knowledge and commandments and, in their individual ways, devote themselves wholly to advancing his glory.

This divine heart is an abyss filled with all blessings, and into the poor should submerge all their needs. It is an abyss of joy in which all of us can immerse our sorrows. It is an abyss of lowliness to counteract our foolishness, an abyss of mercy for the wretched, an abyss of love to meet our every need.

Are you making no progress in prayer? Then you need only offer God the prayers, which the Savior has poured out for us in the sacrament of the altar. Offer God his fervent love in reparation for your slug-gishness. In the course of every activity pray as follows: 'My God, I do this or I endure that in the heart of your Son and according to his holy counsels. I offer it to you in reparation for anything blameworthy or imperfect in my actions.' Continue to do this in every circumstance of life.

*But above all preserve peace of heart. This is more valuable than any treasure. In order to preserve it there is nothing more useful than renouncing your own will and substituting for it the will of the divine heart. In this way his will can carry out for us whatever contributes to his glory, and we will be happy to be his subjects and to trust entirely in him."*

➤

# Sister Rosalind Christian Ministries

S ISTER ROSALIND CHRISTIAN MINISTRIES is a 501(c)(3) nonprofit organization dedicated to the spiritual and physical healing of individuals through healing touch and a closer relationship with God.

Sister Rosalind Christian Ministries accepts cash donations and donations of stocks and securities, real estate and personal property, income-producing gifts, charitable lead trusts, charitable gift annuities, charitable remainder trusts, life insurance, endowments and other charitable giving vehicles. Please call us to discuss charitable-giving options. There can be many tax benefits to including Sister Rosalind's Christian Ministries in your estate planning.

All donations to Sister Rosalind Christian Ministries are tax deductible.

### Sister Rosalind Christian Ministries Goals:
- Spiritual Wellness Centers
- Organized Prayer Groups
- Wellness Products
- Retreat Programs
- Web Sites to Reach Out to the World

### Friends of Sister Rosalind
If you are interested in volunteering your expertise, efforts and/or time to help Sister Rosalind in her ministry, please contact us.

**Sister Rosalind Healing Retreats**

Sister Rosalind is planning to hold healing retreats that combine spiritual healing, healing touch, and other healing modalities. Please call to be placed on our mailing list for these retreats.

Please contact:

*Sister Rosalind Christian Ministries*
149 E. Thompson Ave., Suite 160
West St. Paul, Minnesota 55118
Web Site: www.sisterrosalind.org
e-mail: info@sisterrosalind.org
Phone (651) 554-3013

# About the Author

JOAN HOLMAN has a multi-dimensional background in the fields of psychology, art, business, marketing, media and communications. She holds a Master's Degree in Counseling Psychology from the Adler Institute of Professional Psychology in Chicago, and a B.A. in Psychology from the University of Minnesota.

Joan spent thousands of hours studying human behavior and human potential and combined research in history, philosophy, religion, psychology, art, science and culture to develop and teach her own original "Psychology for Artists" course at the College of Visual Arts in St. Paul, Minnesota. She also had her own private psychotherapy practice, which she called "Psychotherapy for Normal People."

An artist and musician, Joan has been involved in research and development for light musical theater revues and has studied fine arts abroad at the Università Internazionale dell'Arte, a private art school in Florence, Italy.

A nationally recognized Internet expert, business consultant and speaker, Joan is dedicated to helping individuals, businesses and organizations achieve success. She is the creator and producer of the award-winning PBS television program *The Legacy of Achievement*™ featuring the lives and lessons of great achievers. In 2003, Joan founded the Spiritual Cinema Alliance, a nonprofit organization dedicated to the development, production, promotion and distribution of spiritually exalting movies and media programs.

A proponent of a holistic approach to healing involving body, mind and spirit, Joan has researched and personally experienced many alternative healing modalities, from body therapies to energy medicine. She also acknowledges and values the contributions of modern medicine and anticipates an increasing trend towards integrative medicine that combines traditional and complementary approaches to healing.

Joan's motto is: "To make the world a better place, make yourself a better person."